How to Stop Backing Down
& Start
Talking Back

LISA FRANKFORT, PH.D., LMFT
PATRICK FANNING

New Harbinger Publications, Inc.

Publisher's Note

This publication is designed to provide accurate and authoritative information in regard to the subject matter covered. It is sold with the understanding that the publisher is not engaged in rendering psychological, financial, legal, or other professional services. If expert assistance or counseling is needed, the services of a competent professional should be sought.

Distributed in Canada by Raincoast Books.

Copyright © 2005 by Lisa Frankfort and Patrick Fanning
New Harbinger Publications, Inc., 5674 Shattuck Avenue, Oakland, CA 94609, www.newharbinger.com

Cover design by Amy Shoup
Cover image: Getty Images/Photodisc Green
Text design by Michele Waters-Kermes and Amy Shoup
Acquired by Melissa Kirk
Edited by Jessica Beebe

ISBN 1-57224-417-8 Paperback

All Rights Reserved, printed in the United States of America

Library of Congress Cataloging-in-Publication Data

Frankfort, Lisa.
  How to stop backing down and start talking back / Lisa Frankfort & Patrick Fanning.
    p. cm.
  ISBN 1-57224-417-8
  1. Interpersonal communication. 2. Assertiveness (Psychology) I. Fanning, Patrick. II. Title.
  BF637.C45F73 2005
  158.2—dc22

                              2005014373

07 06 05

10 9 8 7 6 5 4 3 2 1

First printing

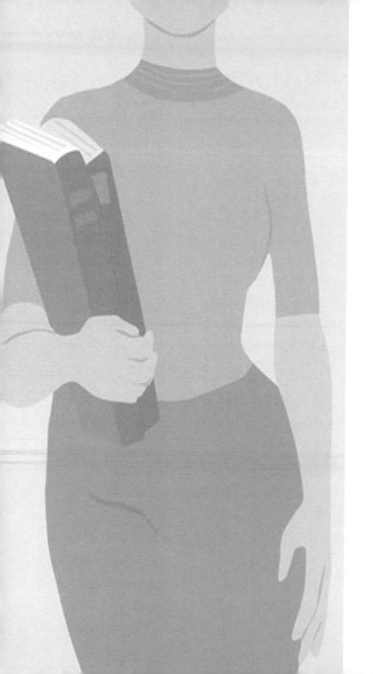

Contents

Part One

Your Personal Bill of Rights

1 Begging Off:
How to Get Out of Nearly Anything

How many times has it happened? Your least favorite acquaintance calls up and asks, "What are you doing Saturday?" You stupidly reply, "Nothing" and then you are trapped into attending a middle school silent auction where you sip flat, warm champagne; bid on a weekend in a time-share apartment in Kraków; and smile smile smile at the bottle blond from the trailer park out by the state highway who wants to prove to you that the cleaning products she sells are not a pyramid scheme.

Rule number one in begging off is *Never admit you have free time.* Repeat this out loud: "I don't know what I'm doing. I'll have to check." As soon as someone hints that they want to invite you to anything, plead ignorance. Find out what the event is, then offer to consult your calendar. This will give you time to answer these crucial questions: *Do I really want to go?* Assuming not, *What's my excuse?*

When it comes to excuses, keep it simple. Don't invent a cousin with multiple sclerosis whom you must move from the hospital to the Hospice Center. Your tormentor will try to co-opt your imaginary prior engagement: "No problem, bring your cousin along. There's wheelchair access, and she can bid on Reverend Sykes's private faith healing session."

The best excuses are short and nebulous: "Sorry, I have other plans" or "I can't come that night" or "That doesn't work for me." Resist the urge to explain how important and unchangeable your prior plans are. This way you are not even lying. Your previous plans may simply be to do nothing but hole up in your apartment with a pint of Ben and Jerry's and glory in your sublime nonattendance at anybody's fund-raiser.

Simple enough, but this approach will not evade the clever interrogator who issues an open-ended invitation that stretches stickily across your entire future like a spiderweb: "We never talk. When can you come over for dinner so I can show you the pictures from my sister-in-law's stepdaughter's home birth?"

In this case, you must never commit. You must insist that you are too busy to even think of setting a date and ask your caller to withdraw the web and reweave it later, preferably after your emigration to Tierra del Fuego: "This week is impossible. I think next week is worse, then I've got to visit my mom, but we haven't set a date yet. Gosh, I'd love to see you, but I'm going to have to get back to you later, when I know what I'm doing."

Note the salient features of what we call the Six-N Response: *Not Now, Not Next, Not Never.* You can't commit now, the near future won't work either, but sometime in the far distant future you *may* notify Ms. Spider of an opening.

Do you call back? It depends. You're certainly under no obligation. Remember, the spider wants to see you, not the other way around. If you feel obliged to meet, set a time and place that allow you to make a quick getaway. Perhaps a bar in the Dallas airport, where you change planes for Tierra del Fuego.

3

2 Sorry, I'm Closed:
Preserving Time for Yourself

You are not 7-Eleven. You don't have to be open twenty-four hours a day, seven days a week, every day of the year. You don't have to be standing at attention in your bow tie and red vest, ready to greet every customer with "How may I help you?"

You have a right to some downtime. You deserve a break from the demands of other people. Your kids/spouse/parents/friends have no right to interrupt what you're doing anytime they need a Ding Dong, Band-Aid, or psychosocial tidbit from you. What would happen if they pulled into your parking lot and found you closed? Would they fall down and die on the spot? No, they'd go to another store or come back another time.

"But people depend on me." Yes, they do—they depend on you like ticks depend on your dog. If you don't cut those bloodsuckers off from time to time, they'll drain you dry.

How to do it? The answer is the assertive put-off. Here are some simple guidelines:

Keep it simple. "I'm taking a break and I can't talk now."

Postpone. "I can't talk about this now. Let's talk after dinner."

Have a special place or a special sign. "When my door is closed, don't disturb me. I'll be out soon, and we can talk then."

Put the worst offenders on notice. "Danny, you're my son and I love you, but I don't want you to call me after ten at night or before nine in the morning."

Create a blacklist of topics. "I don't want to hear about loaning you money, loaning you my car, or doing your laundry."

Simplify. Get off phone trees, committees, discussion groups, and burglar alarm call lists.

Ralph was a talented electronics technician who planned to work on a solar power invention in the evenings after work. But every evening, he'd be interrupted a dozen times by calls from colleagues, family, and friends who wanted his help. Finally he realized that he had to take steps to protect his free time. First he asked people to talk to him at work or call on the weekend instead of during weekday evenings. That helped a little. Finally he removed the shop phone and installed a message machine that said, "Hi, this is Ralph's message line. Please leave your number, and Ralph will call you back." Ralph turned the ringer and speaker all the way down so he wouldn't be tempted to screen calls and pick up when he was in the shop.

If you stop acting like everybody's convenience store clerk, they will stop treating you like one. They will come to think of you as more of a professional, like a doctor, lawyer, or architect. They will treat you like someone whose help and time is valuable—someone who is available, but not 24-7. People will ask if you have time to talk to them now or if you'd rather make an appointment for an extended conversation. You will get the breaks you deserve, and they will get your undivided, cheerful attention when you're open for business.

3 What You've Got Coming to You

Kelly is one of those folks who has no sense of personal rights. She's working two jobs to make ends meet and supporting her husband, Joe, who is voluntarily unemployed and on a quest to be a musician. It has never occurred to Kelly that she has rights just like Joe does.

Kelly developed an idea of what she was entitled to in her life based on some mistaken beliefs, assumptions, and rules that came from the warped mirror of her family. Have you ever looked into a mirror and thought that you didn't look quite right (and we don't mean in the dressing room, trying on a swimsuit)? Some mirrors give back a distorted reflection. You might know there's something amiss with the mirror without recognizing the effect of those distortions.

Sometimes the rules are overt (*Always apologize in order to keep the peace*) and sometimes they are implied (*Don't apply to college, because it would make your brother feel bad*). These ideas are like doors slamming, limiting your life. You might even be told that you are selfish, that you must think you're so special, that you're insensitive, that you shouldn't have talked about your problems outside the family. The list goes on and on.

When you try to obey those rules, you feel depressed and unworthy. Go against them and you feel guilty. You end up surrounded by people who use you to get their own needs met. Works great for them, right? Well, time to kick those guys to the curb.

It may be news to you, but you have personal rights just because you are a living, breathing human being. Are we really sure that you have personal rights? Of course we are. In fact, it says so in the Declaration of Independence. Yeah, we know, you slept through history class in high school. No matter. We're here to refresh your memory. The Declaration says that there are certain "inalienable" rights, meaning they aren't open to discussion. And that these rights include "life, liberty, and the pursuit of happiness." Wow, and you just wanted to know if it was okay to disagree at the dinner table or say no when someone asked you to run an errand on your day off.

Although you're entitled to these rights, you still have to do the work. Here's how. Think about the rules you seem to live by right now, both obvious and hidden. Make an actual list on paper, and you'll probably see how negative and soul-squelching they are. If you allowed yourself the pursuit of your own happiness, what are some new rules that would go on that list?

If you're getting stuck, flip the old rule list and see what happens. For example, if you wrote, "I'm not allowed to talk about what I need," change that around and write, "I have the right to ask for what I need from others." Remember they have a right to say no, but we bet you'll feel differently about yourself even if that happens. And you might be surprised.

Think about how different your life would be if you granted yourself just one or two of these personal rights.

I have the right to be who I am & like me
to stand up for myself
to not be afraid, bullied, threatened

4 The Colors of No:
You Are Allowed to Be Negative

Ever since you first asserted your autonomy at age two by telling your mama "No!" she and the rest of society have been trying to beat it out of you. Contrary, opinionated, strong-willed children are difficult to control, so everybody told you how much "nicer" it was to get along, to be agreeable, to cooperate and play well with others.

Take a moment to get in touch with your inner two-year-old. Remember how great it was to plant your baby feet, spread wide your chubby legs so the training pants wouldn't fall down, push out your lower lip, and scream "No!" to all the unreasonable demands of the grown-up world: *Get up. Go to sleep. Eat your lunch. No cookies now. Change your clothes. Be quiet. Speak up.* Actually, the demands then weren't so different than the demands now, were they?

The big difference these days is that you are now an adult. You have an adult's right to make your own decisions. You have a right to decide how you will spend your free time, whom you will hang out with, where you will go, what you will eat for dinner, and when you will eat or sleep.

Gwendolyn was a baker who worked in a busy bakery. The boss was too cheap to hire enough counter help for busy weekend mornings, so Gwen was repeatedly asked to help out front from eight to ten, after she had baked all night already. She wanted to be nice and to be liked, so she agreed, but she never got enough extra pay or thanks to make it worthwhile. Finally she got so run-down she had to say, "No, I can't do it." Did she get fired? Did the boss hate her? Not at all. The boss just shrugged, asked somebody else, and eventually hired an extra weekend person.

Don't wait until your accommodating nature makes you sick. Start now by asking yourself the key question whenever someone makes a demand on you: *Do I really want to do this?* If the answer is no, practice saying it in ways that fit your personality and get people off your back:

Simple	No.
Polite	No, thank you.
Repetitious	No, no, no.
Profane	Hell no!
Regretful	Sorry, I can't.
Emphatic	No way!
Cheerful	Nope.
Cute	Nosiree.
Disappointed	I'd love to, but I don't have the time.
Frank	You know, I don't really want to.
Blaming others	My boyfriend won't let me.
Military	Negative.
Meteorological	When hell freezes over.
Multilingual	No, nein, nyet, non.
Predictive	Not in a million years.

Part Two

The Three Styles

5 Goldilocks and the Three Styles:
Passive, Aggressive, and Assertive

Once upon a time, there was a young girl named Goldilocks who was lost in the Assertiveness Woods. At first she sat under a tree and cried, but that was too passive. Then she got mad and started kicking the tree, but that was too aggressive. Finally she fired up her handheld global positioning unit and...

You can see where this is going, so there's no need to continue. The point is that the story of Goldilocks is the earliest recorded account of assertiveness training. This thinly-disguised parable was designed to teach that there is always a middle way to the solution of any problem: a "just right" assertive style.

The passive style is the cold mush, the tiny chair, the squishy bed. Being passive is unsatisfying because you don't get what you want. Instead, you spend a lot of time providing others with what *they* want. Carol was the baby-bear type. She sat in her failing antique store day after day, wishing her rent wasn't going up, wishing the guy in the hat would buy the armoire he kept examining, wishing Bill would ask her out, and wishing her brakes didn't squeak. She was too shy and afraid of conflict to protest her landlord's rent hike, to bargain with the man in the hat, to ask Bill out, or to insist that her mechanic redo her brake job. But everyone thought she was a very nice person, when they thought of her at all.

The aggressive style is the scalding mush, the huge chair, the hard bed. Being aggressive is unsatisfying because forcing people to give you what you want backfires in the long term. Your loud, intimidating style alienates those you try to dominate, and they refuse to deal with you anymore. Josh was the papa-bear type. He ran his marriage and his body shop with an iron hand, bullying his wife, June, into going to the Indy 500 instead of visiting her mom in Florida, bawling out his kids for their lousy grades in high school, insisting that his guys work overtime without pay, and intimidating customers into accepting second-rate work. These days you have to be careful around Josh. Don't ask him about his divorce, whether he ever hears from his kids, or why he had to close his shop.

The assertive style is just right. Like the warm mush, assertiveness nourishes your soul by allowing you to express your true opinions. Like the comfortable chair, assertiveness supports you by enabling you to ask clearly for what you want. Like the firm bed, assertiveness allows you to rest easy at night, knowing that you can stick up for your own rights without violating the rights of others. Lillian was the mama-bear type. She had an instinct for finding the middle way between too passive and too aggressive. She could ask the tree surgeon to come back to remove one more branch without charge. She could get her husband to stop leaving motorcycle parts on the coffee table without him going ballistic. She could enforce a lactose-free diet for her son James in preschool. When her son Paul fell off the back of his dad's bike and broke his arm, Lillian managed the busy emergency room doc, her crestfallen husband, and her hypercritical parents—all without screaming hysterically or collapsing in a puddle on the floor. Everybody liked Lillian and depended on her to keep her head, keep her word, and keep her life in order.

13

6 Three Magic Words:
Components of Good, Assertive Expression

When Idina was at college, her mother always asked her, "Do you need anything?" Idina's family had been poor, and Idina believed if she had air, food, and shelter, she didn't "need" anything.

Guy had no problem expressing his wants or his thoughts. "I want you to be responsible," he told his son. "I think that directive is a crock of shit," he told his coworker. "I want you to stop acting like the world revolves around you," he told his sister.

Lizzie believed she was adept at identifying her feelings. On a good day, she was "fine," "okay," or "good." On a bad day, she was "not so good."

So Idina walked around in seven-year-old jeans because they hadn't disintegrated enough that she "needed" another pair. Guy found that his son, his coworker, and his sister seemed angry and avoided him at every opportunity. Lizzie's friends stopped asking how she was feeling.

Each of these folks had problems expressing the three components of good, assertive communication: thoughts, feelings, and wants.

Thoughts. Most of us have a running commentary of thoughts, many of which would not make sense to others. You don't have to think clearly if the only one hearing your thoughts is you. But if you want someone else to respond to you and take you seriously, consider how your thoughts are reflected in what comes out of your mouth. Guy needs to work on being specific without being insulting. "If you leave food out for Sparky to get into, it could make her sick."

Feelings. Expressing feelings is a way for you to give color and richness to your thoughts, a way to clarify the meaning of your experience and share it with others. Lizzie's description of her feelings was the emotional equivalent of beige. If you're not sure what you're feeling, start small and work up from there. Begin with the basic categories—mad, sad, and glad—and then try adding to them. Get out a thesaurus and look up the twenty words for irritated or thrilled. Try 'em on and see what fits.

Wants. Of course Idina would be confused about the difference between wants and needs. A family with money would see a clothing budget as a need, but a family without would label an extra pair of jeans as a luxury. Maybe it helps to see wants and needs as a continuum rather than black-and-white categories. If you are having trouble believing that you have a right to anything that isn't essential to your survival, read chapter 3, "What You've Got Coming to You." Then try saying what you want out loud.

15

Put them all together. "I think that camping this weekend might not be a good idea. I'm worried that we'll get really wet. I want to either put it off until later or just do something different." When you express your thoughts, feelings, and wants, you prevent the misunderstandings that arise when only part of the picture is revealed, and you connect with others by giving them a deeper understanding of your experience.

7 Your Manifesto:
Creating Your Assertiveness Goals

Have you ever made New Year's resolutions? Have you actually kept any of them—past January 3? Maybe you decided to get in shape and went to a spinning class for a month. Then, suddenly, June appeared and...oh well, there's always next year.

Resolutions tend not to work. Although there may be a determination to do something different, there generally isn't a plan. Resolutions are the starting point; goals are the destination. You need a plan of action to get you from the intention to the end result.

You can resolve to be assertive in your life. This is a good thing. Your goal can be to behave assertively in your life. Also a good thing. Oh yeah, here's the hard part: the plan. This is going to require a little work.

First things first. What assertiveness goals would you like to set? As you can probably guess, you're not getting anywhere until you spell that out. Be specific. You cannot get away with saying, "I resolve to be assertive in the office, with Jules, and at home. Okay, I'm done." Nuh uh. Try again.

Ask yourself how you will know that you were assertive in that situation or with that person. Rather than deciding *I'll be assertive about a bad purchase*, try *I'll take the yarn back to the store and ask that they replace the balls that are from a different dye lot.* Rather than writing *I'll be assertive on the phone*, write *I'll tell my friends that I can talk until 10:00 P.M., and then I'll get off the phone.* Make sure the goal is small and manageable. If the goal is large or has several parts to it, break it down into smaller steps.

Wait a second. What's that word in the chapter title? We're almost at the end of the chapter, and there's been no mention of the manifesto. Good observation. Okay, so what is a manifesto and what's it doing in the title? Wasn't "Creating Assertiveness Goals" good enough? Obviously not.

A manifesto is similar to a resolution, with one neat feature: it's public. It's a way to make it known that you want to get somewhere with your assertiveness goals. And why is this a good thing? Don't worry, it's not public like public speaking. It's a way to keep you honest and on task. Once you have written down your very specific goals, starting with easy ones and working up to the more difficult and challenging ones, then you let someone else know about it.

It might be as simple as telling your coworker that you want to tell John not to smoke around you when you're in the lounge. Or you might want to print out a copy of your goals and give it to your brother so he can check in with you periodically. It might also mean leaving notes in the apartment so your honey can see them as well as you. People tend to actually follow through on goals when they are accountable to someone. Think of it as homework for adults. And besides, they are your goals. So say it loud and say it proud. And get to work!

17

8 You Know You're Assertive When...
(An Intuitive Guide)

In this book, you don't have to read or think about your early childhood traumas, your damaged self-esteem, your unconscious beliefs, or any of that tedious self-help double-talk that Freudians call *popsychbulschitzen*.

Want to know the difference between passive, aggressive, and assertive people? Want to know where you fit in those three pigeonholes and where you need to go? Just glance through these three columns and notice where you feel more comfortable.

Passive	Aggressive	Assertive
Porky Pig	Donald Duck	Mickey Mouse
baby blue	fire engine red	forest green
white bread	jalapeño loaf	bran muffin
Mary Tyler Moore	Jack Nicholson	Tom Hanks
Certs	Red Hots	Snickers
Kia Rio	Hummer H2	Toyota Camry
elevator music	heavy metal	jazz classics
Confucius	Nietzsche	Einstein
graffiti	bullhorn	cell phone
Dumbo	Rambo	Jimbo

Passive	Aggressive	Assertive
Lifetime	Fox	HBO
miniature poodle	pit bull	golden retriever
cat	cat	cat

Just to clarify, imagine you have to turn left onto a busy highway with no traffic light. If you come to a complete stop at the stop sign and listen to three songs on the radio before you judge it's okay to turn, you're passive. If you come to a complete stop and hear half a song before turning, you're assertive. If you roll through the stop, turn immediately, and can't hear the radio because of all the honking, you're aggressive.

You know you're passive if you have to look up your own phone number. You know you're aggressive if you know your bail bondsman's number by heart.

What would you do if you walked into your kitchen in the morning and there was a strange dog sitting in the middle of the room? If you're passive, you go back to bed. If you're assertive, you call animal control. If you're aggressive, you kick it out of the way and make some coffee.

19

Part Three

Listening and Expressing

9 All Ears:
Assertive Listening

Even though we've somehow divided men and women into planets—Mars, Venus, and maybe Pluto—the one thing everyone shares is a yearning desire to feel understood. And even if men use fewer words than women, the bottom line is that every person wants a good listener.

What is it that makes for an assertive listener? How can a listener be assertive, anyway? That would seem to be the one area where being passive would work pretty darn good. Well, not exactly.

Mark's boyfriend, A.J., thinks he's a good listener, that he communicates perfect understanding of what Mark is going through. Mark tells a different story. "So, if I say, 'Wow, I had an awful day at work. My boss was a complete jerk and expected me to stay until 6:30,' A.J. will break in and say, 'I know! My boss is a cretin! This is the fourth time he's—' and A.J.'s off and running. He thinks we've connected because we both hate our jobs. I know he didn't hear a word I said. Then I'm in a worse mood, and I think, *Why did I even try?*"

So here are some tips on active listening. Maybe Mark could have A.J. read this, since he's having trouble getting a word in edgewise.

- Listen up, listeners. In order to be an assertive listener, you have to actually shut up for a while. How are you going to know what's being said if you're listening only to the sound of your own voice?

- Listening means more than being silent and counting to twenty so you can start talking again. But if you're completely silent, the other person may wonder if you're still breathing. Sounds silly, but a genuine "yeah" or "uh huh" lets the other person know you're with them.

- Do you hear what is being said to you? If you couldn't repeat the speaker's last two sentences, you probably didn't hear them. Maybe because it's too noisy in your own head. Tune out your own judgments, mind reading, and worries. Otherwise, it's like hearing two radio stations at once.

- Ask yourself why the person is telling you this story. Do they want your opinion, sympathy, or anger on their behalf? Conversations go off in the ditch sometimes when a friend wants you to be supportive and calm and you get caught up in your own feelings of outrage over what happened. Try to put yourself in their sneakers. And if you really don't know what they want from you, try asking.

- Do you understand what's being said? Plenty of people can remember what was said but not know why it's important. If you aren't connecting the dots, gently ask, "What's getting to you about this?"

- If you can, connect those dots. An observation like "So Mya must remind you of your sister" can show that you understand what's meaningful about their story.

23

10 Say It with Your Body:
Nonverbal Assertiveness

Sometimes, you can be misunderstood without saying a thing. In the ladies' room one afternoon, Emma overhead something that horrified her. Alice and Kate, assistants from her office, began discussing their coworkers. Emma heard herself described as someone who "won't even look at you, won't give you the time of day, and never has anything to say to anyone." Clearly, these women saw her as stuck-up.

In fact, Emma was often crippled by shyness and had been that way since high school, when she'd been picked on. Emma thought of herself as a hard worker—she just put her head down and did her assignments until it was time to leave. She had never made friends easily and tended to be on the periphery in any situation. But it didn't mean that she didn't like people or that she thought she was superior. She just didn't know how to show others she wanted a connection with them.

Emma's situation is not unusual. Shy people are frequently misperceived by others because their nonverbal communication is so passive. They might have little expression on their face and rarely use gestures. Sometimes they physically stand further away in conversations, not wanting to take up space. This style gives others very little to go on and leads to misunderstandings.

If you're shy, how can you assert yourself without a total personality overhaul? Here are some simple but effective ideas that Emma, for example, could try:

Maintain eye contact with others. This can be quite hard if you believe direct eye contact is rude. In reality, it's a simple way to let others know you're paying attention.

Be aware of the physical distance between yourself and others. If you're unsure of how close to stand, watch the behavior of others. Many shy people position themselves close enough to hear but far enough away to be unnoticed. The problem is that going unnoticed means you are forfeiting connection with others. Yet being noticed for parking yourself a yard away leads others to assume that you don't want to be a part of the group or that you aren't a part of the group but you are eavesdropping. Not a great choice, huh?

Remember what Mom always told you about your posture? Stand up straight and square your shoulders. This creates an open and inviting stance. If you walk around with hunched shoulders, staring at the carpet, chances are you might be the only one to notice that quarter on the floor, but you also will not feel great emotionally. Changing your posture can help you actually feel more positive.

Stay connected. Even if you feel tongue-tied, you can still let others know you are listening and responding. Lots of facial expressions give that impression: smiling, nodding in response, eye rolling, and laughing all keep you a part of things and keep others from making unwarranted assumptions.

Now you can be assertive without even opening your mouth!

25

11 Just the Facts, Ma'am:
Getting to the Point

Lance was a district manager who really liked his employees. He had a small problem, however. His schedule was packed, and getting his employees to come to the point was like herding cats. Originally, he saw this as their problem, not his.

"They leave me such long messages that my voicemail cuts them off! C'mon! Stop rambling! At meetings they go off on tangents, and I feel trapped into nodding and smiling like a plastic dog in the rear window of someone's car, but inside I'm thinking, *Oh my God, we haven't gotten to half of the agenda items.* My dentist told me I cracked a tooth from gritting my teeth."

With a little practice, Lance altered the dynamic between himself and his employees. Try this yourself and see if you can't protect your disappearing natural resource: your time.

- Think about which interactions are problematic. Is it that people can clearly identify what they want but seem to believe that a request worth stating once is worth repeating three times? Or are people unclear about what they need? Does the speaker wander off into irrelevancies and tangents? Or do they mix their work requests with comments about that ball game last night (which you missed anyhow because you were on the phone)?

- Communicate clearly yourself. If you are vague, unclear, or diffuse, others will take this as permission to mirror you. Set the tone for the conversation.

- Avoid saying things you would otherwise say to encourage the speaker to talk more. When you want others to engage more fully, you ask open-ended questions, ask them to tell you more, ask for their opinions. When you want just the facts, ma'am, ask questions that require a yes-or-no response. Watch your tendency to say things like "Yeah, yeah. Uh huh. Wow. Really!"

- Set limits that show the problem bearer your goal is to help. Make the best use of everyone's time, but don't shut people down so they can't tell you the important stuff. Try saying, "Let me stop you here and see if I've got this down correctly" or "I need to know if I understand (your request, what you need, the reason for your call)."

- Telegraph why you are setting the limit and why it helps you to help them. It is okay to stop someone if you need clarification or you can tell they are going off track. "I'm going to interrupt you here, Kim. I'm in traffic with a big rig behind me, so I'm concerned about missing something. Tell me exactly what you need about the shipment, and I'll get back to you once I've gotten off this freeway."

Rather than grinding his teeth to dust, Lance started communicating strategically. He stopped others in order to clarify their requests and repeated a revised version, ending with "Have I got that right?" He then said what he would do about their need, punctuating this by saying, "Great!"—in effect congratulating both of them on having finished another agenda item. He maintained his good relationships with his employees and his sanity. And he saved on those dental bills.

12 Me, Me, Me:
Using I-Statements

There's more to assertive expression than just shouting, "Me, me, me," but that's a good start. Actually, start with "I" and you're on the right track. I-statements are at the heart of assertive expression.

I-statements are your desires, feelings, and opinions expressed with "I" at the beginning of a short, honest sentence. When you use "I," you take responsibility for the feeling or opinion or request rather than foisting it on someone else. You talk out of your own genuine experience, without blaming others, guessing at their motives, or calling them names.

It's really all about pronouns, those pesky little words that stand in for real people, places, and things. It's easy to wimp out and use the third-person pronouns "one," "they," "he," "she," and "it" as a way of ducking responsibility for your own true opinions:

Bad	Better
One should be careful whom one trusts.	I don't trust your brother.
They say Cadillacs are good cars.	I really want the Cadillac.
It's a long way to Boston.	I don't want to drive all the way to Boston.

On the other hand, some people use the second-person "you" like a club to bash others:

Bad	Better
You're irresponsible, lazy, and oversexed.	I was alarmed when your rent check bounced, and I'd like you to do more around the house than just try to jump my bones every half hour.
You hurt my feelings.	I felt insulted when you said I was unreliable.

It's also about grammar. It's hard to be assertive when using the passive voice, which allows you to have action without an actor:

Bad	Better
Mistakes were made.	I made a mistake.
The letter was mailed late.	I mailed the letter late.

Finally, avoid the fake I-message that puts a happy "I" face on the aggressive "you" club:

Bad	Better
I feel you are too bossy.	I feel resentful when you tell me how to wash the dishes.

If you are careful to express yourself using "I" instead of all the other pronouns, you will be well on your way to a more assertive style.

13 Drama Queen for a Day:
Practicing Spontaneity

In the fifties and early sixties, instead of feminism, they had a TV show called *Queen for a Day*. Some deserving wife and mother would be nominated by her family to receive a little overdue recognition for her years of domestic servitude. She'd be flown to Hollywood, treated to some new clothes and a hairdo, then taken on a TV studio tour, where she'd be "surprised" by being ushered in front of the cameras and declared Queen for a Day.

She'd get a lot of attention and testimonials, plus a bunch of free stuff from the show's sponsors—mink stoles, automobiles, trips, and appliances. The show was judged a success if the queen could be repeatedly reduced to a fetching state of simultaneous tears and laughter.

For weeks those queens had been practicing how to cry and laugh at the same time and make it look spontaneous and convincing.

The point of this TV Land nostalgia fest is that all good drama needs rehearsal. How much reality do you think there is in today's reality TV, anyway?

Do you have a dramatic confrontation coming up in which you stand to win or lose something important? Something big—like your freedom, a new house, a great job, a new Edsel, or a Norman of Hollywood mink stole? If so, you need to rehearse.

Everybody mentally rehearses what they plan to say before they say it, but we mean something much more dynamic. Think of asking for a raise, bargaining with your landlord for new drapes, or proposing marriage as a scene you are playing in a TV show.

- Write out your lines in dialogue form.

- Include what you think the other people are likely to say.

- Prepare a good comeback for every question and objection.

- Practice your lines in front of a mirror. This is the most important part!

- Keep rehearsing until you are letter-perfect, relaxed, and natural.

- Schedule the show by setting a time and place to talk.

- If appropriate, recruit "sponsors"—people to go with you and be on your side.

- Show up on time and put on your show.

Amber knew her husband, Jake, would freak out when she told him she wanted to go with her cousins on an all-girl trip to Atlantic City. So she wrote out her opening lines carefully, using I-statements to separate her thoughts, feelings, and wants clearly. She was very careful not to sound like she was accusing Jake of being boring, cheap, or jealous, although he definitely was all three. She prepared comebacks for all his likely cheap, boring, jealous objections. She practiced in front of the mirror, pretending to be Meryl Streep or Jodie Foster. She got her cousin Joelle to come over on Saturday afternoon when Jake would be in a good mood, and together they put on a show so moving that Jake was reduced to simultaneous tears and laughter, unable to say anything but a choked "Have a good time."

14 **Personal Slogans:**
Affirmations for Today

The Charmin Toilet Tissue division of Procter & Gamble is dedicated to "Making Potty Training Easier for You and Your Cub." Hostess offers "Affordable Nutrition for the Whole Family" on their "Planet Twinkie" Web site.

In this corporate age, every doofus group—however heinous, obvious, or trivial their mission—needs a mission statement. They use slogans, jingles, tag lines, brand names, and all the other tricks of advertising to secure a hold on your attention.

To anchor yourself in this sea of commercial noise, you need some personal slogans of your own. In a kinder, gentler age, these slogans were called "affirmations." Whatever you call them, they serve to remind you of your own agenda, put you back on course when you wander, and protect you from the negative campaigns of the culture, your family, and your own doubts. They also help you clarify your values, zeroing in on what you need to do to become more assertive and less passive or aggressive. Make your slogans short, simple, and positive in tone:

- I have a right to put myself first sometimes.

- I can forgive myself for my mistakes.

- My feelings are legitimate, and I am their final judge.

- I have a right to express my own opinions.

- I can change my mind when I need to.

- It's okay to ask for help when I need it.

- I can change what I don't like.

- I don't have to take everyone else's advice.

- I have a right to say no.

- My time is my own.

- I am responsible only for my own problems, not other people's.

- When I'm in pain or unhappy, I can say so.

[handwritten margin note: I like me / I'm a great person / This is mine, that's yours / My 4 words]

Come up with two or three slogans that sum up the changes you are trying to make. Write them on Post-its (a 3M Company product with the slogan "Always ready to help"). Stick them where you will see them frequently: on your bathroom mirror, above the Charmin, on your computer monitor, in your cupboard next to the Twinkies, and in your wallet or purse.

Before you go to sleep at night and when you first wake in the morning, recite your slogans to yourself. Use your slogans to dispel the negative self-talk that haunts your mind. When other people criticize or impose on you, use your slogans in conversation. Tell your boss, "My time is my own. I have a right to say no if I can't stay overtime." When your dad says you should "snap out of it," you can say, "My feelings are real and legitimate. I'm the final judge of how I feel, not you."

As a last resort, try saying, "I'm just trying to make potty training easier for you and your cub." Use the moment of stunned silence to gather your thoughts or bug out.

33

15 Talking to Yourself First:
The Empty Chair Exercise

Have you ever thought that the key to standing up for yourself might be muzzling other people? Have you ever fantasized about telling someone off while they were gagged so they couldn't interrupt? Have you ever thought, *Who am I kidding? I don't even know what I meant to say?*

The empty chair exercise is a method for you to figure out what you'd like to say and practice assertiveness all by yourself. It can help you identify what you think and feel about a situation you'd like to deal with or how you could confront a particular person. You do this by talking to them as if they were actually in front of you.

Marianne was upset with her longtime friend Anita, who had been talking and laughing with Marianne's boyfriend, Mick, at a party. Not even sure why she was so mad, she retreated into glaring. Anita didn't get the point, but she got cold and snippy in response. Soon they weren't even speaking.

When she first tried the empty chair exercise, Marianne felt really awkward and self-conscious, but she felt committed to figuring this out. In talking aloud, Marianne discovered that it wasn't that she thought Anita was making a play for Mick; it was that she felt Anita really preferred Mick as a friend over her. She was jealous, but not in the way she had thought. Talking to the empty chair got her to a place of clarity, when before she had felt blank and angry. It enabled her to finally approach Anita and say clearly that she felt ignored and hurt that her friend maybe didn't find her as interesting or fun as she once had. Anita was shocked and dismayed, and they made a pact to spend more time, just the two of them, repairing their friendship.

- Set up two chairs facing each other. Do this at a time when you won't be interrupted. Sit in the first chair; the other chair is for the person with whom you are having an issue.

- Close your eyes and think about the situation in question, making it as vivid as you can.

- Identify what you believe the problem to be and any feelings that you're aware of.

- Explain the problem and your feelings about it to the person in the empty chair. The great thing about this exercise is you have time to sort this out.

- Tell the person in the empty chair what you want from them. You can try out different responses, at both passive and aggressive ends of the spectrum, without any fear of attack or reprisal. It's a wonderful way to vent and blow off steam, stare daggers, or cuss your heart out. You can even throw a magazine.

- When you've told this person in the empty chair what you want in many different ways, you can decide what you think your best option actually is. If you want to try the advanced technique, sit in the other chair and imagine how they might respond. That will prod you to think of ways to further the dialogue between the two of you.

Give yourself some practice at what you really want to say, and then go see that real person.

16 Truth as Strategy:
The Honest "How Are You?"

How many times have you been asked, "How are you?" and answered "Fine"?

Does the banality and insincerity of this ritual drive you nutsy? If so, strike a blow for candor and enjoy the cheap thrills of the honest "How are you?"

When you allow yourself to answer the formulaic question honestly, it opens up vast regions of subject matter ranging from the tragic to the humorous. Just imagine how your routine would be spiced up if you answered like this:

Interpersonal

Terrible. My husband is cheating on me.

Desolate. Nobody loves me.

I'm lonely. Want to be my friend?

Psychiatric

Terrible. I've been depressed since 1987.

Which of my multiple personalities are you addressing?

I'm okay, except when the homicidal rage kicks in.

Medical

Not so good since the biopsy results came back.

Still working on the projectile vomiting.

Dying to talk about my surgery. Sit down and get comfortable.

Philosophical

Every day, in every way, I am getting better and better.

Enjoying the absurdity.

Being here now.

Pharmaceutical

Balancing my meds with some success.

Great since the ecstasy came on.

Lousy. My pot connection died of emphysema.

Political

Wishing I was Canadian.

Doing my best to finance the government.

Not bad for a bleeding heart liberal.

Vulgar

Great, just had a humongous bowel movement.

Dying to get laid.

Can I bum some Viagra?

37

17 Screenplay:
Writing Scripts for Yourself

Angela's creative side had her whiling away the day imagining dramatic scenarios: She'd forgotten the iron was left on and had come home only to be stopped by the firemen, who shook their heads and said, "Gutted. Totally gutted. Nothing but ashes." Or her husband of eighteen years saying (as the roof fell into flames behind him), "I'm leaving you for Oona, my secretary. Now that she's gotten her bachelor's degree, she needs the guidance and wisdom of an older man. Plus, she says I'm hot." Or that Angela was the only one who knew that the councilman had cheated her town out of a million dollars and she was going to expose him.

In her own melodrama, Angela wrote all the parts and shot endlessly to her own satisfaction. In her real life, she had stage fright whenever she had a phone call to make. Without endless chances to yell "Cut!" and have another go at it, she was paralyzed. Initially, Angela believed that having a vivid fantasy life was more entertaining than inquiring about how to get a sticker for her car that would allow her to park legally on her block. But she realized that having the car towed a third time was a drama she was willing to live without.

Suggesting that Angela use her script-writing skills, her therapist transformed Angela's tendency to daydream into a useful skill. At first, Angela felt like a dork deliberately composing dialogue for such simple situations. She thought the words should just flow naturally. Her therapist pointed out that any good scriptwriter did rewrites so the actors' words would sound natural while having the desired impact.

Here's how you can write a script to make that necessary call:

- On a pad of paper, write out what you need to know. Is it who is responsible for fixing the potholes on Seventh Avenue? Or the number of tickets allowed for family members for your son's choral recital? Is it how to get an upgrade on a car you rented? A name, a number, or how to do something?

- Write out your introduction. "Hi, my name is Angela. I'm Kari's mom/your neighbor, blue house on the right/a concerned voter/a subscriber/a potential student."

- Write short sentences stating the purpose of your call. Get your information across in a way that the other person can follow and that won't confuse you. "I need the number for.../to know how to.../to be able to..."

- One reason to keep it brief is that you might be talking to the wrong person. If so, just ask who has the information you need and go from there.

- Now make the call and read your lines, allowing the other person to respond. Breathe while you are listening to keep yourself calm and clear-headed. Feel free to make notes to take away the added pressure of trying to remember later what was said.

At the end of the call, pat yourself on the back and say to yourself, "That's a wrap!"

Part Four
Responding to Criticism

18 Yeah, So?
Acknowledging Criticism

It never fails. When someone criticizes you, however mildly, you regress. Your new boss mentions the importance of punctuality when you are five minutes late. The professor in your graduate seminar corrects you on a date. The guy at the dry cleaners says, "Never eat ice cream in cashmere."

However trivial or unjustified the criticism is, it immediately plunges you back to childhood, when your mom caught you with the crayons in front of the scribbled wallpaper. You feel the urge to apologize, explain, defend yourself: it wasn't your fault, you're sorry, it was an accident, you have a good reason, they don't understand the context, you're doing your best.

You know what? You don't owe everybody an explanation, much less an apology. Before you dissolve into a puddle of expiation, ask yourself:

- Am I actually in the wrong here?

- Am I hurting anybody?

- Does this person have real authority over me?

- Do I really care what this person thinks of me?

- Is this criticism justified?

- Is this criticism constructive?

- Are there any significant repercussions to blowing this jerk off?

If the answer is a resounding no, consider responding with simple acknowledgment: "Yeah, so?" You can elaborate or fancy it up a little, but the message is the same:

- "Yeah, I guess I could be more careful."

- "Oops, my bad." (said with an insouciant, shit-eating grin)

- "That's right, I'm buying a motorcycle and they are dangerous."

- "I agree, I have the messiest room in the dorm."

With luck, the "Yeah, so" approach will take the wind out of your critic's sails and leave the person in becalmed befuddlement. Many critics are just looking for a way to count coup, a way to score points by getting you flustered. When you calmly acknowledge their opening blow and refuse to fight back, it's like coating yourself in conversational Crisco—your opponent can't get a grip.

Consuelo was a masseuse who was very sensitive to any negative feedback from her clients. If a woman told her that she was too rough, or somebody asked her not to talk during her massage, Consuelo fell all over herself apologizing and justifying herself. Her cousin, Beatrice, also a masseuse, took her aside during a slow time at the spa.

"Listen," her cousin said, "You can't take these bitches so seriously. You're just a machine to them, so let it roll off like a machine. You're a good person and a good masseuse. Just say okay and do it different."

Consuelo found that "okay" was all the response she needed for 95 percent of her prickly clients. Her composure, self-esteem, and tips all improved.

43

19 Anything's Possible:
Agreeing with Critics in Probability

Some naysayers are really just consumed with negativity, waiting for the next disaster to occur so they can smugly observe, "Well, I told you that was gonna happen." Even without a degree in the mathematics of probability, they will happily predict any number of bad things that you are inviting because you just won't listen to them. (Of course ignoring them guarantees the disaster; every mathematician knows that probability is not entirely rational.)

Think of it this way. You and your pal there, the critic, are both gamblers, but you are calculating the odds in vastly different directions. The critic says the odds are an absolute sure thing that he's right. So much in his favor that you'd be a sucker to bet against him. You know there's a squeaker of a chance that he's right, but you're betting it's a million to one against. Or you think he could be right, but you just don't care.

Neither of you is going to collect any winnings in any meaningful way, although the critic just loves to have bragging rights, and isn't that in itself nausea inducing? What you really want here is to acknowledge that it's *possible* (in some weird parallel universe) that he's right without sacrificing your self-esteem in the process. So how do you do this incredible sleight of hand?

They say,	"You know, looks are everything for a woman in business. You gotta wear something sexy and get out there and network. You should be hosting cocktail parties, showing off those nice legs. You gotta work it to make it. Otherwise, somebody'll get in ahead of you."
You say,	"Yes, that's entirely possible."
Don't add,	"It's about as likely as having an asteroid fall on your ugly head. Which is just too damn bad, because your head is an affront to humanity."

They say,	"You're too trusting. You can't just go around talking to cab drivers and waitresses and doormen like that. You don't know who those people are. They'll rip you off every chance they get."
You say,	"Uh huh, you could be right there."
Don't add,	"And I predict you'll end up alone and with no teeth."

45

You can nod if you'd like to add a behavioral gesture in order to make this complete lie more believable.

If you want to use bigger words, you could say, "Yeah, it sure is conceivable that could happen" or "Yes, in all likelihood it could go that way."

Leave out "when hell freezes over" or words to that effect.

20 Over and Out:
How to Shut Off Criticism

You can respond to criticism by acknowledging the part that's true, agreeing in principle, and so on. That's okay if the criticism contains a shred of constructive content. But what about criticism that is entirely untrue, malicious, destructive, or manipulative? Those types of critics don't deserve any kind of agreement or acknowledgment. They are sniping at your self-esteem with real bullets and deserve to be cut off at the knees. As in any skirmish, you have three possible moves: retreat, take cover, or counterattack.

Retreat. Often, the best tactic is to disengage entirely: leave the scene, hang up the phone, abrogate the contract, move out, don't answer the letter. The new drummer in Lennie's band kept disrupting their first rehearsal by nitpicking every note Lennie played on his guitar. Lennie was confident in his musical ability, so he removed the irritant in the simplest way: by cutting the rehearsal short, finding a new drummer, and not calling the critical one back.

Take cover. If you can't retreat, then take cover: ignore the critic, refuse to answer, insist on changing the subject, postpone the conversation, dazzle them with BS. Karen was a nursing union rep trying to run a meeting to explain the new hospital contract to the nursing staff.

A radical young nurse asked, "Why is the union doing nothing to promote a single payer system in this country?" The question was so inappropriate and unfair that

Karen took cover behind Robert's Rules of Order (even though their meetings weren't run that way).

"That's out of order," Karen said. "It comes under old business, and it's not on the agenda." Then Karen ignored the guy for the rest of the meeting.

Counterattack. If there's no cover and you can't retreat, counterattack with all the weapons you can muster. Malicious critics are dirty fighters, and they started it, so there's no need to hold back. Attack their logic, their manners, their ethics, their appearance, or their mother.

Jaycee's stepmother said, "That skirt's so short you could go into business for yourself."

Jaycee replied, "You're just jealous because I'd have something to sell, and you've been bankrupt for twenty years."

"Fancy talk for someone who never graduated high school."

"Well, you're awfully rude for someone so desperate for attention."

"I've never been so insulted in my life."

"Stick around. I haven't even called you a dried-up old prune yet. Or we could talk about how you seduced my daddy while Momma was on her deathbed."

At this her stepmother ran from the apartment, leaving Jaycee in sole possession of the battlefield.

21 Splitting Hairs:
The Hypothetical Out

Although you may feel differently, the critic in your life is not necessarily attacking your ability to function in the world or walk around without a keeper. The critic is just someone who always wants to appear as if they have a Ph.D. on every known subject, convinced that you never made it past elementary school. These critics are just plain smarter than the rest of the world and are doing you an enormous favor by bestowing their wisdom on you. Undoubtedly, you will be grateful to them, since you get the benefit of their knowing all this crap. They know you better than you know you. You have a problem, they have a solution. Even if you didn't know you had a problem.

Actually, the problem is theirs, and the solution is yours. Here's what you do: say only half of your answer aloud.

Critic says, "You know, what you really need to do to unclog that drain is pour in a combination of hot coffee, vinegar, cola, and a little ammonia. Because otherwise you're just helping the plumber put his seven kids through college on what he's going to charge you."

You say, "Yeah, if I choose not to tackle the drain myself, I could really be paying a lot for a plumber."

Unsaid: "And I'll need to take out a home equity loan to pay for a kitchen remodel, what with the explosion and all, if I stick all that stuff down my pipes."

Critic says,	"You need to have your kid circumcised, ya know. Because if you don't, then he's going to look different from all the other kids when he's in the locker room and he's probably going to get beat up a lot and then he'll never want to play high school or college sports and he's gonna end up blaming you for being different and you'll have to pay his therapy bills."
You say,	"Yup, if my husband and I make the decision not to have our son circumcised, he might feel different from the other kids, and that would be difficult to deal with."
Unsaid:	"Can I borrow your pocketknife for a second? Now, you just hold still."

Critic says,	"You should wait until the landlord tells you what to clean when you move out. Otherwise you'll end up spending hours cleaning when you could've gotten away with just vacuuming the carpet. They're gonna repaint anyway."
You say,	"You are so right. If I use my weekend to scrub out the kitchen and bathroom and clean the twelve years' worth of dust off the shelves, it could really be overkill. It would be a drag to do all that when my landlord might not even notice."
Unsaid:	"I'd probably catch some horrible respiratory illness from breathing in the spores in *your* apartment."

Remember "If you can't say something nice, don't say it at all"? Your goal here is to not feed the beast. You'll have a G-rated mouth, but no one will know that it's NC-17 in your head.

22 **Please Go On:**
Probing for More Information

Dealing with critical people is usually like a snowball fight. You have to keep your distance, keep your vulnerable parts under cover, and hurl enough of your own snowballs to hold the critics off. You can't really listen or talk meaningfully because you might expose too much and get plastered.

Nevertheless, once in a very great while, criticism can be constructive. If you listen carefully, you can learn something about yourself that's worth knowing. But how do you do this without getting an earful of snow? The technique is called *probing.*

You simply ask the critic to tell you more, without agreeing to what you've heard so far, until you know whether the critic is a helpful friend or an ingratiating spy hiding a snowball. *Tell me more, I don't get it, What do you mean by that?* and *How does that work?* are probing phrases that can elicit more information without giving up the game.

Pearl was complaining to her coworker Meg about their mutual boss, Jason, when Meg interjected, "You're so sensitive."

Pearl's alarm bells went off. Did she mean *too* sensitive? Pearl wasn't sure, so she sent out a probe: "What do you mean by sensitive?" Pearl was asking Meg to define her terms—was she offering a hug or a snowball?

Meg replied, "I mean you really pick up on people's feelings."

Still not sure, Pearl probed again, frankly, "In a good way?"

"Sure. You've got Jason's number. You see right through to his basic insecurity."

Pearl was relieved to find that Meg's criticism was meant to be constructive. However, things could have gone the other way:

Meg: You're so sensitive.

Pearl: What do you mean by sensitive?

Meg: You take everything too personally. You're too thin skinned.

Pearl: Well, it's true I'm very sensitive to others. And right now I sense that I need to get back to work.

Pearl agreed to the last thing she heard that she liked, then ducked back behind her snow fort, better known as an office cubicle.

Probing for constructive criticism can show you aspects of your personality or behavior that you have not been aware of. Just be cautious and remember to duck and cover the moment you feel the telltale chill of snow down your neck.

51

23 The Art of the Blowoff:
Agreeing in Part, Disagreeing in Private

Many times, when people criticize, they use poor communication skills to do so. They are global in their attacks on you, which makes it sound as though you can't do anything right, ever. No way, nohow. Things are rarely that absolute, including mistakes, but you wouldn't know it to listen to a critic. Listen to how they frame their criticism, and you'll hear how they try to paint you into a corner.

Critics use words like "always," "everybody," and "never." As in "You always leave things to the last minute" or "Everybody in the office is affected by how you and Sheila hate each other" or "You'll never understand, no matter how many times you're told." Even if you do procrastinate a bit and Sheila isn't your favorite person and you were confused the first time that got explained—well, there's not much room in there for a qualification, is there?

So, how to deal with this kind of criticism? If you think the feedback is valid, by all means cop to it. But if it just seems over the top and includes sweeping generalizations along with a grain of truth, you've got a decision to make. If the critic is someone you have to keep dealing with, and you don't want to start a battle, here's how to respond:

Scan the criticism. Pick it over as if you are looking for the one good tomato in a basket of squishy ones. Respond only to the good tomato. What you will be saying, in effect, is "I acknowledge that this part of what you are saying has some accuracy to it." You can say,

"It's true that I was late getting to the restaurant."

"Yes, Sheila and I had a fight in January."

"You're right. I didn't understand the instructions."

Get the last word. Depending on the situation and the person who has leveled the criticism at you, you may want to add a little something extra. If you simply want to bring the criticism to a halt, you need only acknowledge the good tomato, the part that was accurate. However, if you want to go further and dispute the quality of a different tomato, you can add your correction. You can say,

> "It's true I was late getting to the restaurant, but I'm generally able to do what I say I'm going to do on time."

> "You're right that Sheila and I had a fight in January, but we've both been quite civil since then."

> "I didn't understand the instructions initially, but I caught on after Ella went over them with me on Tuesday."

This way you acknowledge that the critic is correct, in part, but you are the last word on the subject of you.

53

24 Turnabout Is Fair Play:
Giving and Receiving Feedback

Eve considers herself to be a good communicator. She can point out what Eric's done wrong, clearly and concisely. As long as he's got nothing to say about it. And forget about hearing what she's done wrong. Then the gloves come off.

As a kid, did you hear the expression "Turnabout is fair play"? Well, surprise! It goes for adults, too. If you can't hear assertive feedback from your partner, it's hard to expect them to hear it from you. It's hard to be told you screwed up. It's human nature to defend yourself. And that would be just fine if it actually worked. Be honest, now. Does attack, defense, and counterattack actually work? Think about it, we'll wait.

Now that that's cleared up, here's how to give and receive feedback assertively:

Setting the Scene

- Choose your time wisely. If it's late and you're both fried, set aside a different time to talk. If you're tempted to forge ahead anyway, ask yourself to predict the outcome.

- If you do pick another time, follow up.

Giving Assertive Feedback

- Be specific. Instead of "The way you are at parties really bugs me," try "I feel uncomfortable at parties when you haven't talked to me for a while. I'd like you to check in with me from time to time."

- Stay focused. Don't get drawn into switching topics.

- Don't match the emotion of an upset partner. Louder is not better.

- Acknowledge that your honey's complaint may have merit and agree to talk about it, but only after the current issue is aired.

Receiving Feedback Assertively

- Step up and give the love of your life the attention you want from them—fair is fair, Golden Rule, and all that do-unto-others stuff.

- Stay focused. Don't shift the blame. "Well, when we were in Yosemite, you ..."

- Ask for clarification. This does not mean saying in a withering tone, "You aren't making any sense, you moron" or "You already said that a gazillion times." You can say, "I'm confused. Are you saying that I'm too loud all the time or just at that dinner?"

- Try being an adult about it and cop to your mistakes: "You're right. I did do that, and it really ticked you off. It wasn't my intention, and I'm sorry." If your sweetie goes for the jugular after that, maybe assertiveness isn't the problem here.

It might be better to give than to receive if we were talking about gifts or acts of charity. In a loving relationship, however, you have to do both.

55

25 Speaking of Kangaroos:
How to Change the Subject

How are your hemorrhoids? Why did your husband leave you? Have you been indicted yet? How's that audit going? What did your son go to jail for? Have you ever had a sexually transmitted disease? So, you got a raise—how much?

There are subjects you don't want to talk about, but people will bring them up anyway. Maureen's mother was always probing about her boyfriends' possibilities as husband and father material, while making little tick-tock gestures over her tummy. Maureen's way of changing the subject was to plug her ears, squinch her eyes shut, and sing "Jingle bells, Mommy smells, Daddy is a rat" off-key.

While this might work with jolly old Mum, you'll need more sophisticated tactics to sidetrack other busybodies. There are many ways of changing the subject:

Mundane	I can't believe this weather we're having.
Generous	Enough about me. Let's talk about you.
Challenging	What makes you ask that?
Retaliatory	Did you go to your AA meeting today?
Fantastic	If you could be any flying creature, what would you be—bird, bat, butterfly, or mosquito?
Marsupial	Speaking of kangaroos, how about I kick you in the stomach?
Philosophical	In a hundred years, what difference will it make?

Sublime   I believe God is the Uncaused Cause, the Sourceless Source, the Eternal Beginning. What do you think?

The rules for changing the subject are simple:

Don't react. When asked if you have stopped drinking Sterno, pretend not to care. Shrug, grimace, and say nothing. If your questioner might possess a shred of decency, try saying, "I don't want to talk about that."

Ask a question. Choose something related to the topic you want to avoid, preferably an angle that is deeply interesting to the other party. "Speaking of Sterno, aren't you famous for your cheese fondue? How do you make that?"

Distract your tormentor. If nothing relevant comes to mind, punt. Blurt out the first thing you can think of that might distract. "Been to the ball game lately? How 'bout them _____ (Giants, Packers, etc.)?"

57

Lie. You don't have to tell the truth to a Nosy Parker. "That wasn't Sterno strained through white bread, that was lemon curd on focaccia."

The next time someone corners you at a party and starts quizzing you about your preferences in flavored douches, remember that *anything goes* in changing the subject: stonewall, lie, shriek, bamboozle, flimflam, bedazzle, and stupefy them with your deft verbal footwork. If that doesn't work, you can fall back on actual footwork and try a kick to the stomach.

Part Five

Handling Difficult People

26 All in the Family:
Dealing with Difficult Relatives

Family members who know you best are the people who can hurt you the worst. They are the geologists and the archaeologists of the emotional world. They know all your cracks and crevices and where the bones are buried. And some are just plain mean, which makes it difficult to speak up for yourself. You don't have to get certified or pass an exam to prove you can parent a child or be a responsible and loving sister.

But they get to say whatever they want to, 'cause they're family, right? Wrong. They say this crap because over the years they've gotten away with it. Your relatives either fail to notice your pain or torture you because they enjoy getting a rise out of you. You end up feeling trapped, helpless, and voiceless. You spend a small fortune on therapy and antacids.

Does any of this sound familiar? "You can't take a joke." "You're too uptight, too sensitive." "You make a big deal out of nothing." Then there's the eye rolling and the snickers. If so, here are some tips for handling the reality show that is your family:

- Think *fire drill*. Know where the exits are and plan your escape route. Give yourself permission to leave the scene, and then do it. Make sure you park where you can get out. It's hard to make a quick getaway when you have to ask someone to move their van.

- Decide where you're going to draw the line. This depends on whether you value the relationship with your relative. If you wouldn't piss on them if they were on fire, you won't put up with much. But if you love your Aunt Mandy, who gets nasty when she drinks too much, enjoy her company early on and then place yourself elsewhere later. Don't give her an opportunity to take potshots at you.

- **Identify an ally**. Who can have your back, stand up for you? "Actually, Alex, you do pick on Janet. Let it go."

- **You deserve respect**. If you don't get it, you have the right to respond. Keep it short, simple, and firm. "Stop now." "No." "I won't listen to this." If the verbal battery continues, you can add consequences. "Alex, your (language, behavior, etc.) is unacceptable. You need to stop (yelling, criticizing, swearing, talking about me in front of the kids, etc.) or I will leave." Others may pressure you to give up your position. After all, it's uncomfortable to witness you calling someone out. Hang tough. Draw your line in the sand, give your relative the opportunity to stop the behavior, and then follow up with your consequences.

- **Don't expect to get everything you want in the moment**. If Alex turns away, mumbling, "She always was too sensitive, probably one of those women's things," you have a moment to either pick battle number two ("I am *not* too sensitive, you horrible shit! You come back here and say that!") or let your brother save face (or at least the part of his face you let him keep in your violent fantasies) by beating a retreat. After all, you got him to quit, and everybody in the room knows it.

27 Not My Little Angel:
Assertiveness with Other People's Kids

Howie was asked once what he thought the top stresses of parenting were. After thinking for about three seconds, he answered, "Dealing with other people's spoiled brats and dealing with my energetic but creative children." Everyone laughed, of course, but it was that laugh of recognition. Howie's friends joked that other people's kids were spoiled but their own were individualistic, that others' were brats but their own were expressing themselves—albeit loudly.

It's pretty funny until you're the one being tyrannized. There probably isn't a person out there who can truthfully say they haven't encountered at least one grocery store tantrum, one kid missing their nap on a small airplane, one obstacle-course-in-a-restaurant story. Ah yes, the food throwing, the shrieking, the property damaging, the back-of-your-seat kicking. It's somehow humiliating to feel victimized by someone who is probably a hundred pounds lighter than you.

So what's a person to do? Here are some things to think about before you take action:

Who can stop the behavior? You generally have three possibilities: the child, the parent, or someone who is responsible in a larger sense (the grocery store manager, the airline steward, the restaurant hostess). If there is someone official you can turn to, this is probably the best bet. Quietly going up to the hostess and describing how mashed potatoes from the next table ended up in your hair may encourage her to take action on behalf of all diners. Kids running amok are a problem for waitstaff as well.

What outcome do you want? Do you want the child to stop, or do you not care as long as they do it to someone else or out of earshot? If the high-pitched screaming by the frozen food section bugs you, you could take your cart to the bakery for a while.

Does the emotional outcome matter to you? Do you care if the parent is offended by your tattling on their angel? Does it matter to you if you are perceived as someone who clearly hates children? If the child is creating havoc for you and others, describe the problem and state what you want. "Excuse me. Your child is kicking my chair, and I'd like him to stop it." If the child doesn't stop, you may need to do a little creative escalation. "If you're really unable to control your child, I'll have to ask the steward to switch your seats."

What should your approach be? Do you want to appear sympathetic to the child or parent, or do you simply want to demand that the parent adhere to boundaries? If you can see that the parent is overwhelmed and frazzled, much can be communicated by a sympathetic look or by saying, "You look like you're having a hard time there. I bet they have a Band-Aid at the counter."

63

You do have a right to enjoy your meal or see a movie or drink your coffee without having your experience destroyed by other people's badly behaved kids. There are likely lots of people around you who would applaud you for asserting yourself, even though they might shrink from the task.

28 Enough about You:
How to Shut Up a Blabbermouth

We all know a blabbermouth: the social climber who goes on and on about her husband's job and all the important people they know, the nervous mom who can't stop talking about every little twitch and tremor of her hideously boring children, the aging uncle who can disgust you for hours with details about his latest surgery. Here are a few suggestions for shutting up blabbermouths, or at least slowing them down so you can slip in a few words:

Let them run out of steam. Some people blab to relieve social anxiety. As long as they are throwing up a screen of words, they feel socially secure. If you really need to talk about something important with a blabbermouth, plan to spend three or four hours together. As they get used to you, they relax gradually and run out of steam. Then you can bring up your important topic without interruption.

Use assertive body language. If you're sitting down, stand up. Spread your arms like a Shakespearean actor about to launch into a monologue. If the blabbermouth doesn't shut up, raise one arm and hold up your index finger like a debater about to make a point. If this doesn't work, clamp your hand firmly over the blabber's mouth. You can also try holding your hands over your ears to indicate that you are no longer listening. If you want to be more subtle, break eye contact and look away as if bored and distracted.

Interrupt. Your mother told you not to, but it's the only way to handle a blabbermouth. Try a gambit like, "Oh, before I forget, I need to ask you..." If the more mild interjections don't work, you may have to be blatant, as in, "Hey! Stop talking! *I* want to say something."

When you finally have a chance to say something, the blabbermouth will probably interrupt you before you finish your first sentence. You need to be firm and not allow yourself to be interrupted. Hold up a hand and say, "Wait, I'm not finished. Let me finish before you interrupt." True blabbermouths will not be insulted. They're used to it.

Prompt for the point. Sometimes it helps to literally ask, "What's your point?" This is definitely necessary for blabbermouths who organize their material according to the principle of digression. They wander from one loose association to another and have often forgotten their original point, way back in the dim mists of history.

Throw up hurdles. Slow and distract blabbermouths by interrupting to offer a drink, move a footstool, suggest a move to another chair or room, show a new lamp. Use anything in the immediate environment as a distraction and possible change of subject. You can even shout out, "Did you hear that?" as though there were an explosion in an adjoining room. Since blabbermouths never listen, even to themselves, they'll never catch you at this trick.

Ask specific questions. Don't ever ask a blabbermouth, "How was your trip?" or "Why are you selling your house?" Ask specific, yes-or-no questions to encourage specific, short answers: "Did you get to Florence on your trip?" or "Have you closed escrow yet?"

29 Fear of Letters:
Surviving Authority Figures

You think of yourself as an assertive person. Standing up for your rights with friends or coworkers is a snap. Then you encounter that select group of individuals who scare the living crap out of you. Those people who get you to regress into a compliant eight-year-old. Who are those people? We refer to them as the people with letters after their names: health-care providers.

Jessica runs an office where she supervises thirty people. Known for her straight-forward, no-nonsense attitude, Jessica was on her third DDS (dentist) in two years. "I hate the noise. I hate the smells. I'm a wimp when it comes to pain," she says. "I had a meltdown this time. I started to cry while he was explaining that I had to have something called root scaling. I don't even know what that is, so why would I be upset? What's worse is that when I started to cry, the assistant handed me a box of Kleenex, and she and the dentist just left the room. I felt like an idiot."

Stan's big fear is MDs. "My son says, 'So, what'd your doctor say?' and I say, 'How the hell would I know?' I sit in the waiting room for half an hour, he breezes in, he can't remember my name, I'm so freaked out *I* can't remember my name, and then he says some gobbledygook like I'm supposed to know what the hell he's talking about. I didn't go to medical school, did I?"

People have letters after their names because they have extensive training, but that doesn't mean you have to sign away your right to quality care. Doctors and dentists are people too, some of whom do an exemplary job and some of whom should seek career counseling pronto. Here's what you can do to be assertive with health-care providers:

You hired 'em, you can fire 'em. You have a right to the best information, care, and treatment possible. Even though there may be some limits in this day of managed care, you still should think of the doctor or dentist as working for you.

Bring up your concerns immediately. Here's what Jessica said to the prospective dentist: "I have a lot of anxiety during exams. I want someone who has experience in this area. If you do, then tell me how you would work with someone like me."

Stan realized that he was assuming both that his doctor wouldn't take the time to explain and that he wouldn't understand the explanation anyway. Under stress, Stan couldn't remember all he needed the doctor to know. Here's how you can deal with that problem:

- Bring a cheat sheet listing everything that feels important. In the comfort of your own home, you'll be better able to notice your symptoms and keep track of them.

- Practice being direct and specific. Vow to be accurate and express yourself clearly.

- If the health-care provider isn't clear enough for you, follow up with "Please explain that again" or "I'm not understanding what you just said."

Both Jessica and Stan were surprised that they could take charge and be their own health-care advocates. Remember that the only person who will be hurt if you turn the reins of responsibility over to a doctor is you.

30 The Bad Boss:
Assertiveness for Underlings

At one time or another, possibly right now, everyone encounters a creature known as the Bad Boss (referred to here as BB). Sometimes it appears only during a full moon; sometimes it moves silently around the cubicles, only to spring when the assistant is at the watering hole or grazing peaceably at her desk. Most often, it appears every damn day.

Yet having a bastard for a boss is no joke. You spend a lot of time at work, and having a beast in authority over you threatens your mental and physical well-being. You feel stressed, angry, vulnerable, helpless, anxious, out of control, overwhelmed, and overburdened. What kind of toll does it take when you experience those feelings every day for years? Many people sink into inertia, believing they can't do anything. Others stuff it until they blow. There is a middle ground between passivity and having a nice little assault charge on your previously clean record.

If you want to do more than survive the predatory BB, it can help to study him in his natural habitat. Think of it as your own National Geographic program. Does he treat all workers the same, or do some handle him better? When the BB rants and swears, maybe one of your coworkers says, "I'll come back when you've calmed down." If you didn't take the BB's bad behavior personally, what explanation would make sense? Does the BB lack communication skills? Does the BB micromanage because he's a highly anxious person, and does the bottle of Maalox in his desk prove your theory? Is he afraid of *his* boss?

- Describe the problem in behavioral terms. "She's a jerk" may be true, but it won't make the problem clearer. Try "She wants to know everything I do."

- What do you want to be different? And no, "Stop being a jerk" isn't the correct answer. How about "I want to be able to eat my lunch without interruption" or "I want to be able to give her a summary of what I've accomplished."

- Before approaching the BB, give yourself time to get grounded. Maybe it's being alone in your office, taking deep, slow breaths. Or having a minute with a coworker who can give you a pep talk. Remind yourself of why this confrontation is vital and that you will survive.

- Say you want to try something different. "I'd like to be as effective as possible on my assignments, and I want to keep you apprised. So what I am going to do is give you a summary twice a day so that you'll know exactly what I've done." Or with a BB who expects you to read his mind, "I want to be clear on what you want on this project because I know it's extremely important. I'd like to write down all your directives and give you time to make corrections, so I'll be absolutely sure I will give you what you are looking for."

Remember that half of dealing with a BB is being clear about what you want. The other half is presenting it in such a way that it appears to go in the direction the BB was already headed.

31 Prison Guard or Coconspirator?
Dealing with Subordinates

Eleven-year-old Janelle was left to babysit her little sister, Sophie. She made Sophie clean up their room, wouldn't let her watch her favorite show, hid her purple T-shirt, and made her take a nap when she wasn't tired. Sophie told their mom, and Janelle got into trouble. The next time she had to babysit, Janelle let Sophie do whatever she wanted, including starting a pillow fight that broke a lamp. Again, Janelle got in trouble.

In the business world, the people are larger and they dress up more, but the same power dynamics hold true. You can get in trouble both ways: by being too aggressive and bossy, and by being too passive and permissive.

The aggressive/bossy approach is the classic command-and-control model of supervisor as prison guard. Your subordinates have to show up on time, adhere to the dress code, meet all deadlines, reach all quotas, and fulfill all duties or incur your wrath. Power and control run from the top down. Obedience and respect supposedly run from the bottom up. The problem with this model is that it only works in armies and prisons. You have to constantly monitor every move your subordinates make. You will never get any more from them than the letter of the job description—no initiative, no creativity, no innovation. And the minute your back is turned, they all slack off.

The passive/permissive approach is the more modern, "collaborative" model of management taken to its absurd extreme. Managers and subordinates become coconspirators, enmeshed in each other's private and personal lives to the point that no one is watching the bottom line or thinking about the organization's real mission. The problem with this model is that it only works in sensitivity groups or communes. You lose all authority and control, gaining in return only a vague sense of camaraderie that will evaporate as soon as the performance evaluations are due.

Assertive managers deal with subordinates in a way that is truly collaborative. They give more suggestions than orders. They set reasonable goals, then give subordinates the time and resources they need to meet them. They are friendly but not intimate, fair rather than strict or permissive. They challenge and inspire rather than threaten and scold.

If you are in a position of authority, follow these simple Do's and Don'ts:

Do	Don't
Set reasonable goals and deadlines	Change them arbitrarily
Reward innovation	Ignore good performance
Dine with staff	Sleep with staff
Treat people equally	Play favorites
Obey the law	Cut corners
Keep your promises	Promise what you can't deliver

32 How to Change Others:
Change How You Relate to Them

It's impossible to change other people, right? Isn't that a recipe for disaster? When you hear those classic words, "If you really cared about me, you would..." you can just open the Yellow Pages to Divorce Lawyers.

Expecting people to change probably won't work, but resigning yourself to another's problematic behavior is not great either, so what are your options? Sometimes it's a good idea to tell people flat out what you want so they don't have to guess. But what about people who don't care what you want or who aren't capable of doing it? Or people you don't know well enough to engage in a long and detailed discussion of your deepest desires? Sometimes the way you relate to others can create the behavior change. First, answer these questions:

- What is the problem?

- Who is the target person with the problematic behavior?

- What change do you want?

- What behavior of your own will you change?

Mona wanted her class (target) to come on time (desired change), and somehow people still trickled in five or ten minutes late (problem behavior) even after she insisted they come on time. She decided to start every single class promptly, and reviewed the homework assignment first (own behavior change). If students were late, they missed the explanations. Within two weeks, there were no stragglers.

Shar's mom, Jacinda, hated any question that started with "Mom, can I …?" because sooner or later things disintegrated into the famous declaration, "You *never* let me do anything!" Each wanted the other to change (so both are targets for change for each other). Either Shar just wore her mom down until she gave in, or her mom lost it and said, "If you don't stop whining, you're looking at staying home all weekend." Finally, Jacinda deliberately ignored anything in a tone she didn't like but gave her full attention any time the whining disappeared. And Shar accidentally behaved in a calm and trustworthy manner and found that her mom offered to drive her to the mall.

Nina saw Tom in the coffee shop pretty often. She knew Tom was a nice guy, but she also knew she didn't want to date him and didn't really want to explain it, either. He frequently said hello to her, a hopeful look on his face. Her goal was to be true to her outgoing, friendly self but not encourage him. She chose to smile and say hi back, then immediately break eye contact and go back to reading her paper. She did this every single time he greeted her. Nina was never cold to Tom, and he got the message with his self-esteem still intact.

So, even without a long, carefully worded, logical, rational explanation leaving lots of room for other people's feelings, you can still get people to do your bidding. It's just that they may not know that's what they're doing. And it's okay to leave them in the dark.

Part Six

Special Strategies

33 Broken Record:
Repeat, Repeat, Repeat

This is a special strategy that dates back to the days of vinyl records, when everyone knew what a broken record sounded like. For the benefit of those born in the last twenty-five years, here's the deal. A bad scratch or crack in a vinyl record would often cause the *needle* on the *record player* to play the same *groove* over and over again, sounding like this: "You ain't nothin' but a hound dog…but a hound dog…but a hound dog…" and repeating forever until some *hepcat* or *chick* gave the machine a jolt and knocked the needle into the next groove.

These days we have CDs that skip tracks and repeat a syllable or two forever. But they sound more like a stutter than a repetition of a recognizable phrase. We considered going clinical and calling this chapter "Invariant Response," but that sounded way too rats-in-mazes for a popular book. And the simple title "Repetition" was struck down as too boring.

So you're stuck reading a chapter with the archaic title "Broken Record." The reason we are going on so long about the title is to take up space. The concept itself is so simple that it can be stated in one sentence:

Repeat your assertive request, over and over, until you get your way.

Actually, the sentence doesn't even need the commas, which are only there to slow you down and make the concept seem more complicated. In fact, "over and over" is repetitious itself and could be deleted, since "repeat" implies that you will say something over and over.

The rest of the chapter will be repetitious paraphrases, elaborations, and examples of this basic idea. So if you get it, you can go on to the next chapter. For those who like to see a dead horse thoroughly beaten, here is an example.

Claire wanted a juicer from her local hardware store, which was having a "Buy one, get one free" sale. She didn't want two juicers, so she asked to buy one juicer for half price. The clerk said no, that wasn't the deal. Claire repeated, "I want to buy one for half price. It's the same thing." The clerk said no, it wasn't the same thing. Claire said, "Yes it is. I want one for half price." As the line behind her got longer and it became apparent that she was not going to (a) buy two, (b) buy one for full price, or (c) go away, the clerk finally gave in and sold her one for half price (which he shoulda done in the first place, the jerk).

That's the secret of the broken record technique: Wear your opponent down by your maddening, invariant, inflexible repetition of your assertive request—until it becomes easier to give you what you want than to endure the broken record.

Here's an exercise for those who learn best by doing: on a separate ream of paper, compose a short, simple request, then write it out longhand 10,000 times.

To summarize, for both the readers who are still with us:

Repeat your assertive request until you get your way ✓

34 Creative Escalation:
Situational Assertiveness

Think about passivity, assertiveness, and aggression as a scale from 1 to 10. If you stay at a 1, you haven't really gone very far, but you probably haven't harmed anything or anyone. If you start at a 10, there might be nowhere to go. Except maybe jail. Knowing where your choices fall on the continuum gives you flexibility. As long as you're willing to accept responsibility for the consequences to yourself and others, you have a wider range of options.

Start with being clear about the problem. The vacuum cleaner you bought last Saturday works, per se, but one of the attachments should work better than it does. What do you want? A new vacuum cleaner, a new attachment, a refund? Maybe you just want to adjust to a less than perfectly cleaned staircase.

Sometimes being passive or philosophical can work. If the problem is insignificant or merely annoying, you might want to say, "Oh well, guess I won't do that again" or "It was only four bucks, no biggie" or "At least nobody died."

If, however, you can't just let it go, then move your playing piece higher on the escalation board. Here's how. When you are explaining the problem to the person you need help from, do not spill your Bad Attitude all over them. Be calm, clear, controlled. Do not yell, no matter how pissed off you are. Keep the goal in mind. If your goal is to vent, go scream at the TV. If your goal is to get someone to fix your problem, play nice. If they didn't do you wrong, you can inspire sympathy by saying, "I know it isn't your fault" or "What do you suggest I do?" or "If you were me, what would you do?" If they are the gatekeeper, you want them to open that gate. Do not act mean or crazy, because others naturally close ranks and ears at this point. Their goal becomes making sure you don't reach yours.

Stay clear and calm no matter how often you have to repeat what the problem is. Remember that although you've said this five times to five people, it's the fifth person's first time hearing it. If the next person can't help you, politely but assertively ask who can. By the time you reach the person with power, they may grant you your heart's desire because you've been so reasonable. But you've also been persistent.

If you've tried all that and they will not accommodate you, either you fold and take yourself out of the game or you move your playing piece to the aggressive end. "In that case, I won't be patronizing your store again, and I'll be more than happy to share my experience. Too bad, because Mrs. Johnson was going to be using your services for her daughter Bel's wedding reception, but I think you can forget about that now." Or "Did I mention that I'm on the school board?" Or "Hey, while I've got you on the phone, can you look up the number for the Better Business Bureau? I'll hold." Or "May I have your business card? I want to make very sure I spell your name correctly in the letter to my attorney."

You can still be aggressive with a smile.

35 **Hold On:**
Buying Time to Gather Your Thoughts

Life is full of pauses. "We'll be right back after a word from our sponsor." "The court will take a one-hour recess." "For every four hours of work, we are legally required to have you take your fifteen-minute break." "The score is twenty-eight to seven as we go to halftime."

Breaks are a normal, natural phenomenon, and they are just what you need when you are being pressured for an opinion or a decision. The other person wants you to answer *now*, and you need to collect your thoughts. If you get flustered easily, even a fairly neutral question can throw you off. "I'm taking the lunch order. If we get five people who want pizza, we can get free breadsticks. So, what'll it be?"

Oftentimes, though, the situations are not so neutral. Perhaps you are stuck between several friends who each want you on their side. "And I told Sarah that I thought she was picking on Melanie, and she said she so wasn't doing that and that Ana thought what she said was justified, but you think I did the right thing, right?" Perhaps you are being guilt-tripped into buying something you can't afford. "Can I put you down for buying a table at the fund-raiser?" Perhaps it's an overeager salesperson. "Let me just total this up and we can get started on the paperwork. I can arrange delivery on Monday. Can I have your credit card? And I assume you'll want the extended warranty."

There are different levels of tactical breaks:

The simple pause. Maybe you just need a second or two to refocus. Take a nice deep breath and say, "Sorry ... What?" While the other person repeats the question, compose your answer. "I don't like pizza. I'll have turkey on wheat, no mayo." If you only need a moment, "um," "well...," or "huh" can suffice.

The momentary delay. This is another break you can take with the other person still standing there. Again, your goal is to buy a little time to collect your thoughts before responding. You simply repeat what the other person said, indicating you want to understand before rendering your own opinion. Obviously, this is for something more important than your sandwich. You can say things like "Let me get this straight," "If I hear you correctly, you would like me to...," or "So you're saying..."

The adult time-out. Use this when you don't want to answer right now, either because you don't want to deal with the other person's reaction or because you don't yet know what you think. You can say the following (even if they are patently untrue): "I know you are a patient person, so I'll think about this a little more." "I know you want me to fully consider the options, and that's exactly what I'm going to do." "Thanks for bringing this to my attention. I'll get back to you."

And regarding those salespeople who don't respond to delays, announce before they open their mouths, "I'm not buying anything today."

36 Plug Your Movie:
How to Stay on *Your* Topic

Admit it: You see your life unfold like a movie. Your train of thought often takes the form of a voice-over. You imagine yourself trading quips with Dave or Jay on late-night TV, reducing millions of insomniac viewers to panting anticipation with the clip from your latest film.

Or perhaps your fantasies are more modest. Perhaps your life seems more like a novel, a play, or an article in the *Tampa Bay Classified Gazette*. The point remains that each of us is the star of our own story. We all have something we love to talk about: our children; our garden; our surgery; our relationship with Jesus, the Buddha, or the little silver guys who live under the barbecue.

The problem is that Dave and Jay and all the other late-night hosts are booked up with real celebs. We ordinary folks have to tell our extraordinary tales to mere friends, relatives, and acquaintances—people with poor interviewing skills who are more interested in telling their own stories than in eliciting ours.

To learn how to hold the stage, watch the late-night interview shows. Despite all the jokes, wisecracks, and Hollywood gossip, veteran movie stars always manage to take care of business, plugging their forthcoming movie at least three times. How do they do it? Here are four tricks you can use as effectively as Tom Hanks or Julia Roberts:

Show the clip. Never leave home without photos of your new grandchild, your homebuilt airplane, or your award-winning pumpkin. Store one of your model boats in the trunk of your car, and keep little jars of jam and the community chest donor forms tucked into your purse in case you can steer the conversation around to canning or charity.

Wave the flag. Wear your sailing club T-shirt, the scarf you bought in Italy, or your *Ask me about macrame* button. When someone comments on your attire, it's an invitation to hold forth, at least until the next commercial message.

"That's a funny story." Use this phrase whenever someone asks you a question. Everybody likes a funny story, they're willing to listen because a funny story is short by definition, and they are relatively patient because they're waiting for the punch line. In fact, you'll rarely need a punch line, since someone is bound to interrupt (we said *relatively* patient).

Flash the host. The night Drew Barrymore stood on Letterman's desk and showed him her boobs has become a TV legend. You don't have to go that far, but the perspicacious blond was on to something: nothing grabs attention like daring self-disclosure.

Next time someone asks what's up, don't respond with your usual "Nothin' much. Trying to stay ahead of the housework." Add drama by admitting, "I'm doing a lot of housework as a way of avoiding sex with Larry." You'll still get to complain about how messy the house is and how tired you are, but the psychological hook of sex (or no sex) with Larry will guarantee a rapt audience...and give you something meatier to think and say about yourself.

37 Middle Way:
The Art of Compromise

Being assertive is great. You state clearly what you think, feel, and want, and then you get it, right?

Ben was a cartoonist and skateboarder whose Peter Pan routine was getting pretty hoary at age twenty-eight. His girlfriend, Rose, was tired of clinging to a Gen-X neo-Goth lifestyle. She wanted to remove the matching skull tattoos, save the navel rings for weekends, get real straight jobs, get married, and start saving for a house. She hit Ben with an assertive statement of her thoughts, feelings, and desires, and he moved back in with Lucy, his old girlfriend.

Being assertive isn't enough. The world is full of people who want something different than you, and some of them are just as assertive as you are. The answer is compromise, and being assertive is just the first step in the art of compromise.

To reach the middle way, the perfect compromise, follow these simple steps:

1. State the problem.

2. Make a proposal.

3. Elicit a counterproposal.

4. Reach agreement.

Of course, it's not really that simple. Just stating a problem in a way that won't upset the other party is difficult. The best way to approach conflict is to assume that you and the other party both have legitimate needs and wants. In fact, it's a good idea to say that out loud. Suggest that you work together to find a middle way, a win-win solution that will give each of you a large portion of what you want. This is the groundwork that Rose failed to lay in her little talk with Ben.

In the rest of this book, we've been preaching about making your proposal: stating what you think, feel, and want without blaming, name calling, and so on. Rose had this down pat. But you also have to have in mind your least acceptable solution: the worst outcome that would still satisfy you as better than nothing. Rose had not thought this out, so her assertive proposal came across as an ultimatum, and it scared Ben back into the arms of that little airhead, Lucy.

Eliciting a counterproposal tends to flow naturally from the previous steps if you have done them well. Reaching agreement is the hard part. Usually, it takes several more proposals and counterproposals as each of you delves deeper into what you really want and what you could possibly give up. Rose and Ben got back together eventually, when they both cooled down and could think of compromise. Their compromise involved a job for Ben, but it was at a skate shop. He moved back in, and they agreed to consider themselves engaged to be married in the future. Ben wore long sleeves instead of removing his tattoos and agreed to help fix up the apartment as a baby step toward home ownership. Things weren't moving as fast as Rose would have preferred, but at least they were moving in the right direction.

38 Time-Out:
When You're Too Angry to Be Assertive

When you're too angry to be assertive, you still don't have to be aggressive. You can take a time-out. Gabriela got so mad at her son, Mikey. He was only five, but he knew how to get her. It was like she had a big red button on her chest labeled *Push for explosion*. Mikey gave it a good slam three or four times a day: teasing the dog into a frenzy, piling pots and pans up into a tower and crashing it down, slamming the back door so hard a pane of glass broke.

She tried putting Mikey in time-out in the bathroom, like she read about in a magazine. But she couldn't stand to just leave him to sit quietly in there. She'd be out in the hall, yelling through the door, calling him a miserable, rotten, spoiled brat.

Gabriela was the one who needed a time-out. She was really locking Mikey away so she wouldn't slam him up against the wall. Her therapist helped her figure out that messiness and noise were triggers for her anger—cues that tipped her very quickly from a good, assertive mother to an aggressive, bitchy mother (just like her own mom, by the way).

The solution for Gabriela was to be alert for the first signs of irritation, before she got too angry. Then she would put *herself* in time-out. She'd go into the bathroom or her bedroom, close the door, and take a moment to calm down. She'd tell herself, "Mikey's only five. Five-year-olds are messy and loud by nature. He's not doing it to push my buttons. I can handle it calmly." When she had cooled off, she could let herself out of time-out and suggest a quieter game for Mikey to play without yelling and calling him names.

<u>What sets you off?</u> Someone putting you down? Talking about your family? Suggesting you're incompetent? Insensitive? Selfish? Stupid? What pushes that detonator in your chest? Identify <u>two or three triggers that can make you angry</u> instantly. The next time you experience one, be prepared to put yourself in time-out.

Just say, "<u>I need to take a time-out. I'll be back in a minute.</u>" Then get out of there before you explode. The best location for a time-out is a quiet place away from others, like a bedroom, bathroom, backyard, front porch—wherever you can retreat for five minutes to calm down.

While you're in time-out, counter your usual angry self-talk with a few calming assertions:

Anger won't help here.

I need to calm down.

I can get smarter, not louder.

What's the assertive—not aggressive—thing to do here?

I can control my feelings.

By putting yourself in time-out when you are too angry to be assertive, you can avoid aggressive outbursts that you will regret later, calm down so you can think clearly, and then return to the situation with your emotions under control.

39 Tell Me about Being Abducted by Aliens:
Dealing with the Genuinely Weird

He seemed normal enough when you started talking at that party, so you said sure, let's have coffee. Now you're burning your lips on a latte, trying to finish it fast so you can bug out. You slide your sandaled left foot with its six toes further under the table as he continues to explain that he is on a mission from God to track down and kill mutants.

Dealing with the genuinely weird has its attractions and its dangers. Interesting people are interesting because they aren't like everyone else, a characteristic they share with weird people, which makes the two types difficult to tell apart sometimes.

When the conversation enters the Woo-Woo Dimension, just ask yourself these two questions: (1) Is this weirdo interesting or boring? (2) Is this weirdo safe or dangerous? Your answers to these questions determine what you should do.

	Interesting	Boring
Safe	stay	change the subject
Dangerous	be careful	leave

Stay if your weirdo seems interesting and safe. Hang in there and ask questions. What else did the alien say? Did Madonna let you keep the bra? How do you milk one of those snakes, anyway? Does your implant get AM or FM?

Change the subject if your weirdo is boring and safe. This probably won't work, but common decency obliges you to try it once. After that, see "Leave" below.

Be careful if your weirdo is both interesting and dangerous. That's the fatal attraction of weirdness—it's so interesting you want to hang around and find out more, but before you know it, you're tied to the bedpost wearing nothing but a tinfoil tiara. Stick to public places and don't sign anything. You know the drill: do everything the innocent victim in the average miniseries thriller should have done.

Leave if the weirdo is dangerous and boring. Forget about politeness or plausibility. Stand up right this second, say, "I hear my baby crying" or "My mother's on fire," and leave.

Disclaimer: Some people act weird because of a physical or developmental disability that affects their appearance, posture, or speech. These folks deserve your kind attention and are not genuinely weird. Genuine weirdness involves wacko beliefs, unusual obsessions, peculiar mannerisms, and deviant behavior that the weirdo has consciously chosen to reveal and could choose to hide. If you can't tell the difference, disregard this chapter and just be nice.

89

40 Know Thyself:
Assertive Introspection

Sounds like it should be obvious, but many people aren't very self-aware, even down to knowing whether they prefer blue over green or vanilla over chocolate. Sometimes families at the Dysfunction Junction do not encourage kids to know themselves, and sometimes they actively discredit or minimize. Some people are only too happy to jump in and tell you all about yourself.

"Oh honey, you don't want that shirt, that's tacky looking."

"You're not angry, are you? You can't be. That would be really childish of you."

"We don't think that way in our family, mister."

Lack of self-awareness can make life confusing and can stall your assertiveness. How can you stand up for yourself when you don't know what you want?

As a kid, Kirk looked forward to accompanying his dad on Saturday errands. But then there was the time his dad took him to Kaplan's Bakery. His dad told him to pick anything he wanted, and Kirk carefully considered every cookie, the Boston cream pie, each cupcake and sugared doughnut. Then his dad looked at his watch and said, "Hurry up, Kirk. I've gotta get to the grocery before two. C'mon now!" Kirk got queasy, although he didn't know why, and he frowned and said he didn't want anything. His dad heaved an exasperated sigh and bought him a jelly filled. "Stop sulking," his dad said in the car when Kirk didn't eat the doughnut, just squished it in the bag. After that, just walking by the bakery made Kirk's insides get all funny.

There are many reasons you might not know what you want. Maybe you are looking for the right answer as if there truly is one, maybe you've been told what you feel, and maybe you've gotten the message that you don't count. Becoming aware, waking up, is the first step.

- Give yourself space to learn about yourself. Maybe you can't label your feelings right away. Maybe you just know that you get a headache when someone makes a categorical statement like "You can't possibly be friends with a Republican." It's not the categorical statement that's giving you a headache; it's someone informing you how you should be.

- Maybe you disagree, but you don't know what you do believe. Start from where you are. Give yourself permission to have opinions or to change them. Start with "I'm not sure I agree." Move on to "I don't agree with that," then ask yourself what it is that just doesn't sit well with you.

- What would you like to change? If the situation could be different, what would you want? Don't judge yourself for it. Let yourself just be.

- Treat yourself as you would someone you've just met. Be friendly and interested and put your (self-)judgments aside. Your only goal is to get to know yourself better.

If you've had a long history of others answering for you or telling you what you think, you need to start simple. Say out loud, "I hate jelly-filled doughnuts. I want a piece of Boston cream pie." Now get yourself to a bakery and practice!

41 My Favorite Cause Is Me:
When It's Okay to Be Selfish

What do you care passionately about? Most times we care deeply about other people or causes but fail to work as hard to stand up for ourselves in a minor key. Some people find it easy to get others to give their time, energy, or money for a cause they believe in—maybe selling chocolate bars at five bucks a pop to finance the sixth-grade class trip to Yosemite. Maybe it's raising hell to protest cigarette sales to minors or collecting a thousand signatures to force the city to put a speed bump at the top of your street.

Have you ever considered that those fund-raising or advocacy skills might be useful on the home front as well? It might not save the whales, but it can work to your advantage. Maybe you want to get your neighbor to return that lawn mower, your roommate to locate that chemistry textbook she borrowed, or your sister to cough up the money she got off you last February. You can even get people to do you a favor, volunteer to help you out, drive you to the airport.

Okay, so what skills do you need to stump for your favorite cause, you?

- Be energetic, not apologetic. "I'm really sorry to ask, but..." doesn't work in politics, and it won't get the workmen to stop parking their truck on your lawn. An enthusiastic "Hey! How're ya doin'? You got a minute?" as an opener works decidedly better.

- Think through why they should care about this, why they should do what you want. Any good fund-raiser has to anticipate resistance, avoidance, the desire to be noncommittal, and engage in the preemptive strike: "I know what you're going to say; you're going to say _____. Well, here's what I would say to that."

- What's in it for them? Give them a reason to hand over that check or pull out that lawn mower. You'll stop badgering them to death, you will stop whining (even if you aren't whining, the promise not to whine is very compelling), they won't be risking the loss of your friendship over something as petty as a broken hair dryer, and you just know how much they value your friendship! You should also think of some not-so-nice consequences if they are foolish enough to turn you down. "Gosh, that's really unfortunate. I won't be able to afford your daughter's raffle tickets, since I was counting on that money you owe me" (accompanied by a soulful, deeply regretful look).

- Congratulate them for making the right decision. Say, "I just feel so good about us" or "I feel a renewed sense of faith in our ability to solve problems." Consider giving them a big hug. Your sister might give you a strange look over your odd behavior, but so what, if you've got a check in your hot little hand.

93

42 Imitation Is the Sincerest Form of Flattery:
Assertive Role Models

How do we learn how to behave in the world, what to say and do? Where do we learn that we have rights, needs, and wants and that we are entitled to ask for these things? Parents are generally the first role models. Later on we collect other role models: that humanities teacher, certain classmates, best friends, the swim coach. All of these people leave their mark on us, for good or bad. Maybe you're missing a good role model because your experience has been more about what you *didn't* want to learn or know about.

Ginny never learned about assertiveness from her family. She learned to talk about current events but not the fact that her brother teased her and broke her toys. She learned to just change the subject if something embarrassing happened. She learned to be passive.

Arieta learned that one wrong word and you were lucky to get out of the house without being hit in the head by a flying ashtray. The kitchen floor had shards of broken dishes and cups still in the corners, gathering dust from countless fights. She discovered that if you wanted attention, you'd better learn to shout louder than the person across the table. You didn't trust anyone, because they were all out to get you.

So how were they to counteract the long history of passive, passive-aggressive, hostile, and mean role models? Ginny and Arieta figured out what they wanted to be like and then looked around to see who might be a likely candidate.

- Learn to observe, not merely react. Pay attention to everything: how a mom handles her child's tantrum in the supermarket, how someone apologizes for treading on another's toe. How do your friends behave toward their partners?

- Identify your difficulty with assertiveness. Do people arriving in a movie line cut in front as if you're invisible? Does your coworker take credit for your innovation? Or do you sound strident and defensive when you voice an opinion? Who around you handles these situations the way you'd want to? Don't stop there. Ask yourself how they do it better. What do you see and hear?

- Borrow phrases from others; use their body language, their gestures and intonation. Be an actor playing the part of an assertive person. Nan's cousin Connie always seemed able to get out of boring conversations, while Nan stood for hours being talked at. She used to say, "That would never happen to Connie," but then she really watched her cousin. Connie would pat the person's shoulder or arm, give them a big smile, and say, "I have to stop you." Just that. She'd give a reason—she had to leave, or go talk to John, or pick up her daughter, or get a sandwich. But the point was, she did what she wanted to do, just because. Instead of seeing Connie as special and herself as unlucky, Nan saw her cousin as a role model.

Even if at first you don't feel it, you can behave your way into asserting yourself.

Part Seven
Special Situations

43 No Strings Attached:
Rejecting Offers of Help

Here's one of the trickiest situations that a student of assertiveness will encounter: negotiating the boundary-bashing, limit-leaning, stop-sign-smacking offer of help. Not just any offer of help, but the one antacids were designed for—the gift, the loan, the just-in-the-nick-of-time assistance with a hopelessly tangled web of strings attached. "I'm happy to babysit every day. You know I love my grandchildren." "Sure, I'll drive you to work every morning." "We'll pay for your tuition, honey. That way you can concentrate on your studies."

How great! How wonderful! How thoughtful! Except there's *always* a catch. "Let me help you out financially. Pay me back when you can" turns into "I support you and you're not grateful" (because you won't marry the person I picked for you or move next door). If you turn it down, it becomes "You don't need me. You've hurt my feelings." And, of course, "I'd love to babysit" entitles them to tell you how you should raise your own children.

Here are some important things to consider:

- How close are you to the person making the offer? You may choose to accept the strings to maintain the relationship. Or you may decide that the consequences will be too much when you look down the road a bit. Just how willing are you to sacrifice your sanity?

- Do a preemptive strike. Offer something in exchange to discourage them from accusing you of using them (though they may do this anyway).

Offer it with energy. "I've got a great idea! Since you so graciously took the kids last weekend so I could study, I'll take yours to the zoo with us. What's good? Thursday? Saturday?" You must be willing to offer it and offer it willingly. If they turn you down, hey, you did offer, and they turned you down.

- Suggest that you are doing them a favor by turning down their offer. Make it sound like accepting it would lead to terrible things, some of which you can reveal, some so awful you can only hint at them. "Oh, I just couldn't let you do that. When I say yes to stuff like that, I get insomnia just thinking about...and I...oh God, you don't even want to know! Thanks, but it's just...better this way."

- Okay, here's the hard one. (We know, they're all hard.) However enticing the offer, you may have to do without. Yup, that's right. Yes, your parents are overinvolved and controlling and think that just because they got you that car, they have the right to demand you be their chauffeur. Yes, your brother got you an incredible, maybe not so legal deal on that leather coat, but now he thinks you're the person to call at 4:00 A.M. from jail. If you are going to cry to your cousin about your terrible problem with your bills, she is going to give you financial advice. Sometimes it's important to just say no to the ties that bind. All offers of help have a price tag. Some are an unbelievable bargain, but some are the equivalent of buying a fifty-dollar chair that costs you a thousand in interest. You may like that chair, but is it really worth it?

44 Put the Cuss Back in Customer:
Retail Assertiveness

Most businesses realize that good customer service is crucial. But once in a while, you run into someone who just doesn't get it, and you need to put the cuss back in customer. Here's how:

State the problem. Cite simple facts, without exaggeration: "I bought this lamp thinking it had the green shade like the one in the showroom, and when I got it home, it had this clear one."

Say what you think. "Whether it's the manufacturer's, the architect's, or the subcontractor's fault, I think it's up to you as the general contractor to make sure the skylights don't leak."

Say what you feel. Here's where a little cussing can go a long way: "I am royally pissed off that you would choose life insurance for me and my family based on which company pays you the highest commission."

Say what you want. "I'd like you to bring us fresh cups of coffee and not charge us for the crème brûlée."

Issue an ultimatum. Most businesses fall under city, county, and state regulations, so this is worth a try if you know whom to call: "If I don't get all my money back with interest, I'm filing a complaint with the (state banking commission, county health inspector, city fire marshal)."

Wear them down. "Let me explain one more time, in more detail so you'll understand."

Here is how Pam put it all together, talking to her auto mechanic about her Jetta:

Pam: (*stating the problem*) I paid you $1,200 to stop my car from vibrating and drifting to the right. You fixed the vibration, but it still drifts to the right.

Mechanic: We did everything you ordered—new struts, ball joints, alignment, balanced the tires.

Pam: (*stating what she thinks*) I didn't ask you to do those things in particular, I asked you to fix the drift to the right. You either messed up one of those repairs or didn't diagnose the problem right.

Mechanic: I've done front end work for ten years. I don't mess up simple stuff like this.

Pam: (*stating what she feels*) Well, maybe it's not a simple problem then. The point is, I'm feeling ripped off here. I've paid top dollar, I've been without a car for two days, and now that I've got it back, I'm scared to drive it.

Mechanic: I don't know what to say.

Pam: *(stating what she wants)* You don't have to *say* anything. What I want you to *do* is take the car back and give me a loaner until you fix it right.

Mechanic: I don't have a loaner.

Pam: What about that Honda I see parked over there all the time?

Mechanic: That's my car.

Pam: *(issuing the ultimatum)* Fine, I'll take that. You can drive mine until you figure out how to fix it. If you can't fix it, I'm going to tell my friends who come here what a lousy job you did.

Mechanic: Okay, okay. Take the Honda. I'll try to have your car fixed by five tonight.

45 Keeping Mum:
When It's Best to Say Nothing

They say silence is golden. For Selena, it was also silver, platinum, and diamond. She wrote an article for her school paper about runaway teens and drugs, based on interviews she had conducted while volunteering at a shelter downtown. She was contacted by a county social worker, a vice cop, and two families of runaways. They all wanted more information so they could help, arrest, or find teenagers who had talked to Selena in confidence.

Selena stalled the social worker, stonewalled the cop, and told one family that they were mistaken about the identity of one of her sources. Then she made the mistake of taking pity on a working mom who missed her troubled daughter so terribly that Selena just had to suggest where the girl might be found. A week later, Selena heard that the girl had been severely beaten by her mom's boyfriend.

With all the emphasis on talk in this and other books, it's easy to forget that sometimes the perfect rejoinder is none at all. You have a right to keep your own counsel. Many questions do not deserve answers. It usually depends on the questioner. Your answer to "Have you ever had a sexually transmitted disease?" will vary depending on who's asking: Your gynecologist? A new lover? Your best friend? A casual acquaintance? A stranger?

You have a right to keep silent when any verbal response would be too embarrassing, offensive, harmful, dangerous, or legally compromising to you or to people you care about. You have the right to say nothing to

- anyone who asks trick questions, such as "Are you still beating your kids?" or to people who ask impertinent questions

- crazy people who accost you on the street

- anyone at whom you are too angry to control what you say, or anyone who is so angry at you they can't listen

- stalkers, obscene phone callers

- people asking about matters under litigation, or anyone who has a restraining order on you

- arresting officers, reporters

- anyone asking about a secret you have promised to keep

Here's how to say nothing:

- Look down to break eye contact, or turn away.

- Get some distance. Leave if possible, at least turn your back.

- If you stay, assume a closed stance: folded arms, crossed legs, head down.

- If you must speak, say "No comment" or "I will not talk about that."

- If forced to say more than "No comment," go on at length about how you can't think of anything to say that will help the situation, so you have chosen to say nothing.

46 Accepting Kudos:
Gracefully Acknowledging Praise

You might not think of accepting a compliment as assertive behavior, but assertiveness is about standing up for yourself, and accepting a compliment is a way of doing just that. So what happens if you don't accept those kind words?

Here's something we bet you haven't thought about. What about the givers of those compliments you're so intent on defusing? While you're busy warding off the evil eye attracted by the compliment, the other person is frustrated and even hurt because you are dismissing a verbal gift.

Genuine compliments are a way to form a connection. When you refuse a compliment, you are rejecting that connection. How do you feel when your officemate congratulates you on being employee of the month and you dismiss the words as if you were offered a rotten orange? Do you feel close to that person? Do you feel good about yourself? Probably not.

If you have difficulty accepting kudos, you may be making negative comments in your head and responding to them rather than to the compliment. Maybe you parry the compliment with tactics like distraction, the defensive volley, minimization, and self-deprecation.

Compliment:	"What a lovely color on you."
Negative self-talk:	*I should never wear pink. Mom always said my skin is too sallow.*
Distraction:	"Uh, did I return that book you loaned me?"
Assertive response:	"I really do love pink."

Compliment:	"You know, I admired the way you explained to Mr. Santiago how the whole process could be streamlined if we reorganized the committee."
Negative self-talk:	*I can't believe how I went on and on. She probably thinks I'm a know-it-all.*
Distraction:	"Thanks! But I really admire how you pulled that project together."
Assertive response:	"Thank you. I really felt that reorganizing would be to everyone's benefit."

Compliment:	"You're the best. I so appreciate your support."
Negative self-talk:	*Am I so special because I listened to her problems for half an hour?*
Distraction:	"It wasn't anything at all. It isn't a big deal. Really."
Assertive response:	"I was happy to do it. I'm glad I was able to help."

Compliment:	"I've learned so much from you. I was lucky to have had you as my teacher this semester."
Negative self-talk:	*Poor thing. If he thinks I'm a good teacher, the rest of them must be awful.*
Distraction:	"Wow, I fooled you, too, huh? That correspondence school degree really worked."
Assertive response:	"It means a lot to me that you had a good experience in my class."

A good starting point in accepting kudos is to simply take a breath, smile, and say thank you.

47 Your Inner Brat:
When It's Okay to Be Bitchy

In the eighties and nineties, it was fashionable to get in touch with your inner child, an earlier version of your personality that various childhood traumas have wounded and stuffed down into your unconscious. But sometimes it makes more sense to get in touch with your inner brat, a scrappy, suspicious, independent version of yourself that has been smothered under knee-jerk niceness. By tapping this primal source of self-interest, you can find the courage and energy to confront the morons of the adult world.

Your inner brat can help you summon up the innate bitchiness you need when

- you're being mistreated

- being nice hasn't worked

- it's the only way to get someone's attention

- you have a legitimate complaint

- you're actually trying to piss people off

- you need to shock yourself out of passivity

Let's say the drapery cleaning guys reinstalled your drapes a week ago. The drapes seemed shorter and more wrinkly than before, but you signed for them and wrote a check despite your misgivings. You've been stewing, and you want to call and make them let out and iron the drapes. For a call like that, you must be in touch with your inner brat. Follow these simple instructions:

1. Lie down on your back on the couch with your arms and legs uncrossed. Close your eyes and relax by taking a series of deep, slow breaths. Clear your mind of all thoughts, including the drapes. Scan your body for tense muscles, and relax any you find.

2. Imagine that you are going down an escalator, down through time, sinking slowly into your past. Imagine yourself getting younger and younger. Stop when you are four or five years old.

3. Imagine a time when you were four or five, some time when you were very disappointed. It could be when you didn't get something you wanted or had to do something you didn't want to do. See yourself in that scene, getting more and more angry and unhappy. Watch yourself having a tantrum, screaming, yelling, turning blue, throwing things.

4. When you can see yourself clearly, imagine merging with that child. Become yourself at age four or five. Feel the rage and power of your brattiness. Enjoy the freedom of letting go in a full-blown tantrum.

5. When you are full of that bratty feeling, open your eyes and make that call. Remember, you can draw on the power of your inner brat whenever life mistreats you.

48 Phone Wars:
How to Leave a Message

These days, when you dial the phone, you're much more likely to get a machine than a person. When you leave a typical recorded message, your chances of getting called back are slim. Phone tag has become a viciously competitive game for the nimble of mind and the assertive of tongue.

The key to winning the phone wars is planning ahead. Don't dial that number until you know

- what you want to say, including all pertinent facts and dates and numbers;

- what questions you must get answered; and

- your preferred outcome.

When you leave a recorded message, use the format below so that if you are cut off by a stingy chip, the most important part of your message will have been recorded:

- name

- number

- date and time

- subject

- what you want (most important parts first)

Of these items, what you want deserves some careful consideration. You don't just want a call back, since the other guy will probably get *your* machine and you'll be it again, back where you started. Before you call, imagine the conversation you want to have and leave a message that asks all the pertinent questions and gives all the necessary information to answer them.

Here's a bad message that will probably result in several frustrating rounds of phone tag: "Steve, this is Chris. I'm thinking of coming over this weekend. Give me a call." Here is the same message, skillfully redone: "Steve, this is Chris. 555-8234. Calling Tuesday morning at nine. Hey, can I come over and see your new boat trailer between nine and ten on Saturday? I want to take some pictures of your hitch setup. Call me and let me know if you'll be there, or if the trailer will be in the driveway where I can get at it without you having to be there." In this version, Chris is more likely to save himself days of phone tag and get his trailer pictures on Saturday.

Create urgency by giving a deadline for the call back. Increase your chances of receiving the call by saying when you will be home to answer the phone. Or give your cell number (and remember to take your cell with you and turn it on).

With recalcitrant phone taggers, try using *preemptive assumption,* a sneaky tactic perfected by investigative journalists. You set a deadline and assume a particular answer if the deadline passes without word from the other person.

- "The *Post* would like to print President Nixon's response to the Watergate piece, which we will need by 6:00 P.M. to make our Tuesday deadline."

- "If I don't hear from you by the second, I'll assume it's okay to fax the report."

- "Unless I hear different from you, I'll paint your Lexus Passionate Pink on Thursday."

111

49 Please Go Out with Me:
How to Ask for a Date

What does assertiveness have to do with a meaningful relationship? Love happens at first sight, right? If it's meant to be, then you won't need to make your desires known. The truth is that many singles are quite risk averse, or they blunder in like the proverbial bull in a china shop.

Here's how the inability to assert yourself with prospective lovers sets you back. Some people refuse to put themselves out in any way, then conclude that no one is out there for them. Or they are taking risks, thank you very much, but no one's interested in a real relationship. Of course, they have to shout this observation over the din of happy hour, hoping that Mr. Right will come buy them another Cosmo and then want to get hitched. Or they make their intentions known by a gentle and subtle inquiry such as, "Hey baby. Wanna get naked?"

Justin is a sweet, intelligent guy who really does want to get married. When he talks about having kids, he gets tears in his eyes. So why isn't he married? Justin says he hasn't met anyone at work. Well, duh. Of the twelve other people in his office, seven are in relationships, one just isn't interested, and four are over fifty.

He plays basketball every Saturday morning with his buddies. Saturday evening he cooks a lovely dinner and eats it in front of the tube, alone. Sunday he is at the coffee shop down the street, reading the *New York Times* so he'll be well informed in case the woman of his dreams wants to discuss politics. He doesn't look up for over two hours. He is practically guaranteed to ride off into the sunset alone.

- Review your dating behavior and be ruthlessly honest. Are you the passive type? You can't complain that you didn't meet anyone this weekend when the truth is you didn't *see* anyone this weekend because you never left the house. Are you the aggressive type? If others respond as if you haven't bathed in two weeks, you may be coming on a bit too strong.

- Are you unsure of how your message is getting across? Ask for feedback from a close friend. Justin's friend said, "Buddy, you look like you're waiting to catch a plane. You look everywhere except at the woman you're with."

- What's stopping you from asserting yourself with someone you are interested in? Can't think of an alternative between silence and dragging someone back to your cave? Try low-key but straightforward. Start with "Hi." The average person will not say, "What do you mean by that?" Ask, "Would you like to get a cup of coffee next week?"

- Beware of the critical commentary in your head. You might be interpreting "I can't this week" as *She doesn't like me* when it really means *I can't this week.*

Many people are afraid to do without the game playing, the beating around the bush, the double entendres, afraid that if they are honest and straightforward, they will be vulnerable when the inevitable rejection occurs. That could happen. Rejection happens a lot. But if you don't want to continue on your path alone, the risk of reaching out may just be worth it.

113

50 Have You Got Mail, or Has Your Mail Got You?
E-mail Assertiveness

Mary cringed whenever she heard the musical "You've got mail" notes on her computer. Her job running a volunteer center for a coalition of local charities made her a slave to e-mail. It poured over her like Niagara Falls from three inexhaustible sources: the deserving but needy clients, the well-meaning but flaky volunteers, and the generous but self-important philanthropists who funded the agency. Her friend Jane had a similar problem. Jane's Web site on collectible dolls generated a lot of repetitious e-mail, which she got tired of responding to over and over. Mary and Jane went out to coffee and brainstormed six napkins' worth of ideas for e-mail assertiveness:

Think before hitting the reply button. You aren't morally obligated to reply to every cretin who has you in his address book.

Write, don't talk. E-mail is so easy that people write carelessly, like they talk. It takes six e-mails to plan a play date that could be settled with one. Plan ahead. Write important e-mails in your word processor, where you can outline, draft, edit, and rewrite more easily. If you have a long list of questions, number them to help the respondent reply thoroughly.

Use smart subject lines and e-mail addresses. They are all your recipient sees before opening (or deleting) your e-mail. Don't miss a chance to communicate assertively.

Jane got better responses from her doll collecting e-mail when she changed her address from *jfmeyers* to *janesdolls*. The perfect subject line summarizes the topic and asks for action in three or four words:

> Your Wednesday assignment

> Where's my refund?

> Doll ships June 8

> URGENT: signature needed today

I want, I think, I feel. The usual formula for a complete, assertive request is to state what you feel, think, and want, in that order. In e-mail, do include your thoughts and feelings, but put the *I want* first, so that it will appear in the preview window.

Make them respond. Give a deadline. Consider using a preemptive assumption such as, "If I don't hear from you by the thirtieth, I'll assume it's all right to harvest your kidney."

Use form letters and stock paragraphs. Create a folder on your hard drive where you can store paragraphs or whole e-mails that you find yourself writing over and over. You can insert them into your e-mails where needed, saving time and improving your effectiveness.

With e-mail, what you don't do is as important as what you do. Don't use all caps—it's like shouting in someone's ear. For emphasis, use asterisks or underlines. Don't use four-letter words. Nobody likes a flamer. Avoid sarcasm. Because e-mail lacks tone of voice and body language, sarcasm is frequently misunderstood. Don't use too many smileys or abbreviations.

Lisa Frankfort, Ph.D., LMFT, is a psychotherapist in private practice and clinical coordinator of Haight Ashbury Psychological services in San Francisco, CA. She holds a doctorate in counseling psychology and has been a licensed marriage and family therapist since 1991. She is coauthor of *The Community-Building Companion.*

Patrick Fanning is a professional writer in the mental health field and the founder of a men's support group in Northern California. He is the coauthor of eight self-help books, including: *Messages: The Communication Skills Book, Self-Esteem, Thoughts and Feelings,* and *Couple Skills.*

Some Other New Harbinger Titles

Talk to Me, Item 3317 $12.95

Romantic Intelligence, Item 3309 $15.95

Eating Mindfully, Item 3503 $13.95

Sex Talk, Item 2868 $12.95

Everyday Adventures for the Soul, Item 2981 $11.95

The Daughter-In-Law's Survival Guide, Item 2817 $12.95

Love Tune-Ups, Item 2744 $10.95

Spiritual Housecleaning, Item 2396 $12.95

The 50 Best Ways to Simplify Your Life, Item 2558 $11.95

Brave New You, Item 2590 $13.95

Loving Your Teenage Daughter, Item 2620 $14.95

The Conscious Bride, Item 2132 $12.95

Juicy Tomatoes, Item 2175 $13.95

Facing 30, Item 1500 $12.95

Fifty Great Tips, Tricks, and Techniques to Connect with Your Teen, Item 3597 $10.95

The Well-Ordered Home, Item 321X $12.95

The Well-Ordered Office, Item 3856 $13.95

10 Simple Solutions to Panic, Item 3252 $11.95

10 Simple Solutions to Shyness, Item 3481 $11.95

The Self-Nourishment Companion, Item 2426 $10.95

Call **toll free, 1-800-748-6273,** or log on to our online bookstore at **www.newharbinger.com** to order. Have your Visa or Mastercard number ready. Or send a check for the titles you want to New Harbinger Publications, Inc., 5674 Shattuck Ave., Oakland, CA 94609. Include $4.50 for the first book and 75¢ for each additional book, to cover shipping and handling. (California residents please include appropriate sales tax.) Allow two to five weeks for delivery.